U-Boats
in action

by Robert C. Stern

illustrated by Don Greer

**U-Boots-kriegabzeichen
(Submarine War Badge)**

squadron/signal publications

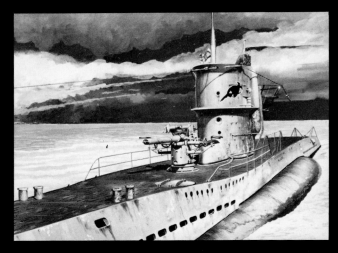

(Cover) Riding on calm water, the deck watch of a mid-war type VIIB scans the horizon for targets. The crew is bearded because the lack of available washing water made shaving a very low-priority item on a U-boat. The "Smiling Sawfish" insignia on the side of the tower is the emblem of 9. Unterseebootsflottille based at Brest.

Photo Credits

All photographs so marked are from Bundesarchiv, Koblenz. The remainder are from the author's collection.
ISBN 0-89747-054-0

Author's Note

This book is the first in what is hoped to be a long series of Warship in Action books from Squadron/Signal. Being part of the "in Action" series, the emphasis is on physical description and individual histories rather than attempting an overall view of the U-boat war. As such this book fills, to the author's knowledge, a hitherto vacant niche in the literature on this subject, a type-by-type survey of those boats that saw operational duty with the Kriegsmarine, explaining their development and success or failure in meeting the demands of war.

If you have photographs of the aircraft, armor, soldiers or ships of any nation, particularly wartime snapshots, why not share them with us and help make Squadron/Signal's books all the more interesting and complete in the future. Any photograph sent to us will be copied and the original returned. The donor will be fully credited for any photos used. Please send them to: Squadron/Signal Publications Inc., 1115 Crowley Dr., Carrollton, TX 75006.

What it was all about, sinking merchant ships! In this case, U-123 (type IXB) makes a surface daylight attack on the British steamer SS Culebra, using its 105mm deck gun in order to conserve precious torpedoes. Such attacks were safe only in areas with no aircraft patrol, as the presence of a guncrew on deck made a crash dive impossible. This incident occured on 25 January 1942 during the Paukenschlag (Roll of Drums) off the U.S. Atlantic coast, an area devoid of anti-submarine defences. During this operation, U-123 under Kapitänleutnant Hardegen sank nine ships on its way to becoming the sixth most successful U-boat of the war. (Bundesarchiv)

Introduction: The U-boat War

The story of the U-boat campaign in World War II is a drama of rise and fall, and almost rise again. The German U-boat arm rose from the ashes to become the Third Reich's most effective weapon against the West. For a few brief months the U-boats seemed to be winning the Battle of the Atlantic, bringing England slowly but surely to her knees, until May 1943 brought a sudden reversal of fortune and the anguish of a losing struggle fought with diminishing resources against a materially superior enemy.

The Versailles Treaty, in an effort to render Germany incapable of waging another World War, prohibited her from possessing submarines, which had so nearly defeated England in WW I. Yet it took less than three years for the Reichsmarine to secretly circumvent this restriction. In July 1922, the "Ingenieurs-Kantoor voor Scheepsbouw", a Dutch ship design and construction firm, was acquired to act as a cover for the clandestine Submarine Development Bureau. The acquisition was made using so called "Black Funds", (monies deliberately over-appropriated by the German Armed Forces for secret use, ie: the same source that financed the Reichswehr's secret armor development in Russia). Among other, more innocent projects, the Dutch-based firm oversaw the design and construction of the boats that were to be prototypes for the U-boat classes that Germany took to war.

The rise to power of Adolph Hitler spurred the German Armed Forces into feverish, if still secret, expansion. The first official U-boat establishment was the "Unterseebootsabwehrschule" (UAS) set up in October 1933. Officially an anti-submarine warfare school, it served mainly as a gathering point and planning center for U-boat personnel. Plans soon emerged for the development of a clandestine U-boat fleet, in similar manner as Göring's secret Luftwaffe, during 1934. Parts were ordered abroad for U-1 through U-24, to be smuggled into Germany in early 1935.

Secrecy, however, was not necessary much longer. On 16 March 1935, Hitler publicly renounced the military provisions of the Versailles Treaty. U-boat construction now proceeded openly and at breakneck pace. This was further legitimized by the signing, on 17 June, of the Naval Agreement which allowed Germany 45% of Great Britain's submarine total, or approximately 45 boats (twice the number then being planned). U-1, a type IIA coastal U-boat, was commissioned just 12 days later. Such was the pace of construction that by January 1936, 12 boats were in commission. By June, 24 had been launched (U-1-U-20, types II A&B; U-25&26, type IA; U-27&33, type VIIA). In September 1935, the first operational structure, 1. Unterseebootsflottille "Weddigen", was set up under Kpt. Karl Dönitz. A veteran of WWI U-boat service, Dönitz was quickly plying Grand Admiral Raeder with theories as to why the U-boat had failed in the Great War and how it could succeed in the next. Already he had developed the strategic insights into how a submarine offensive could defeat a maritime enemy, and the tactics this required: Tonnageschlacht (Tonnage War) and Rudeltaktik (Wolfpack Attacks).

The origin of Germany's World War II U-boat designs was in a series of boats built for other nations to German plans. Seen above are three submarines of the Finnish Navy, Vetehinen, Vesihiisi and Iku-Turso (Left to Right). Built in 1930-31 to a design originating at the Dutch-based Submarine Development Bureau, the Vetehinen class boats were experimental prototypes of the later medium-size, type VIIs. Tested by German crews before being turned over to the Finns, they provided the designers with much valuable information during a period when Germany possessed no submarines of her own.

The theory of Tonnageschlacht is an exercise in logic. In order to defeat England (the presumed enemy of a U-boat War), Germany must sink more merchant shipping than the enemy can replace, for long enough to economically strangle her. Therefore, the real (and only worthwhile) target of the U-boat is the merchant ship, and the only tactical question is how to sink the greatest number with the least loss of U-boats. Dönitz theorized that Germany's WWI boats were ultimately unsuccessful because merchant convoys were only a secondary target and, more importantly, because once a convoy was sighted, any attack was unco-ordinated, made by the sighting U-boat only, submerged and in daylight. Yet, as Dönitz was aware, a submerged U-boat was a slow, nearly blind, inefficient weapon.

The Rudeltaktik was a plan to overcome these weaknesses. Dönitz envisioned packs of 6 to 9 boats, spread out in a sweep formation, working across the Atlantic. Once a convoy was sighted, the sighting boat proceeded to act as a beacon to the rest of the pack. Once gathered, the pack would attack on the surface at night, when a U-boat's low profile made it practically invisible and its surface speed of 15 kts made it faster than a convoy's average of 7-9 kts, and as fast as most anti-submarine escorts. The U-boat was to submerge only to escape pursuit after an attack. Daylight was spent moving ahead of the convoy on the surface for the next night's attack.

To make this work, Dönitz wanted a large fleet of medium-size, maneuverable, reasonably inexpensive boats (the type VIIs). He fiercely opposed the construction of large, expensive, long-range, "fleet-type" raiders favored by most other navies. By his figures, 300 medium boats were the minimum required to give successful results (100 on station, 100 in transit and 100 training or refitting).

Considering the pace at which U-boat construction began, this goal did not appear unattainable. Yet, haggling over which type of boat to build (the naval staff favored fewer, large U-boats) and deliberate deception by Hitler (his approval in 1938 of the Z Plan, a long-range naval construction plan calling for only 129 U-boats by 1946, disapproving a short-range plan that would have made more, sooner) put Dönitz' aim of 300 boats far beyond reach. By the time the Z Plan was dropped in late summer 1939, the damage had been done. Even though a new plan was then adopted, projecting 300 boats by mid 1942, Germany went to war with just 57 U-boats, with only 26 being the ocean-going type VIIs and IXs.

39 of these boats were at sea, on station around England, when war broke out. But after the initial attack, rarely were more than 7 boats in action at any time. The boats, of necessity, acted individually. Yet successes did come because England proved to be equally unprepared for the war. Convoys were in effect only 100 miles west of Ireland, escorts were so few in number that at times only two were available for each convoy and air surveilance was effective only in the Channel-North Sea area. The Rudeltaktik was tried experimentally for the first time with a pack of three boats in October, being found to work. Before all U-boats were withdrawn from the Atlantic in April 1940, 224 ships of 1.3 million GRT were sunk.

Weserübung (the invasion of Denmark and Norway), for which the U-boats were needed to help protect against Royal Navy interference, proved to be a frustrating, if educational, experience. Faulty torpedoes, particularly the magnetic detonators, cost the boats many victories, but corrections were put in hand. It proved most valuably that another of Dönitz' contentions were correct. The 1940 vintage submarine was simply too slow and vulnerable to be effective, with consistency, against well-protected war-ships.

The period that followed, between July 1940 and December 1941, came to be known as the "Happy Time" or the "Fette Jahre" (Fat Years). This was the time of the great U-boat Aces, of Prien, Schepke and Kretschmer. It was the time of the first fruition of Dönitz' plans, as a much delayed wartime construction program finally brought results. The institution of such a program was put off again and again by Hitler as if he were afraid of the consequences. Yet this delay may well have lost Germany the war. Considering the results obtained by the handful of boats available in 1940, had the increased production of 1941-42 come a year earlier, as it could have, the Atlantic could well have been made untenable for the British.

The "Happy Times" were made possible, to a large degree, by the capture in June 1940 of the French Atlantic ports. U-boats no longer had to dodge the RAF-patrolled North Sea, but had open Atlantic access through the Bay of Biscay. While the number of boats was never high (Christmas Day 1940 there was one U-boat in the Atlantic), pack attacks began almost immediately. In September 1940, 10 boats attacked two convoys sinking 16 ships, and in October, 12 boats converged on convoys SC-7 and HX-79 for four successive nights, sinking 32 ships totalling 154, 661 GRT. There could be no more doubt, the wolfpack worked. Monthly tonnage sunk reached as high as 350,000 GRT, and for the year was over 2,300,000 GRT.

Successes continued unabated into 1941. They were helped along by the slowly increasing number of new boats coming into service (11 boats commissioned in January 1941 as opposed to one in January 1940). By Spring 1941, with still only about 120 boats in service, Dönitz was able to set up regular sweeplines of up to 10 boats, to search the convoy routes for targets. By September, it was not uncommon to have 2 or 3 groups in the Atlantic at any one time.

Yet in spite of this, successes fell short of 1940 figures. The primary reason was the increased efficiency of Britain's anti-submarine measures. The acquisition of 50 old US Navy Destroyers in September 1940 helped the Royal Navy over the immediate crisis. The agreement by the US to take over convoying in the Western Atlantic was even more helpful. Yet, perhaps most ominous for the U-boats was the increasing effectiveness and range of RAF aircraft flying West of Ireland and South of Iceland. The U-boats were being forced away from the coast of England, out into the open ocean. Further, the capture of U-110 and weather ship Bremen (and their code books) allowed the British to break the back of the German mid-ocean supply system. Between 28 May and 15 June 1941, 10 weather ships, supply ships and tankers were sunk.

Ominous too, was the loss of the three great U-boat aces in a period of just 10 days. On 8 March 1941, Kptlt. Gunther Prien, the "Bull of Scapa Flow", and U-47, was lost while approaching a convoy. On 17 March, Kptlt. Joachim Schepke was killed when his U-100 was rammed and sunk, and Kvtkpt. Otto Kretschmer, the leading ace with 266,629 GRT and one destroyer sunk, was captured when U-99 was forced to surface on the same day. Yet, the end of the "Happy Times" came not as a result of Allied action, but of a naval staff decision. In an attempt to keep supply lines open to North Africa and prevent the Torch landings (and over Dönitz' vigorous but futile objections), 20 U-boats were moved into the Mediterranean, based at La Spezia, and most of the rest were stationed in the vicinity of Gibraltar. In spite of a great drop in sinkings at the end of the year, over 2,100,000 GRT were sunk in 1941.

The entry of the US into the war reversed the downward trend, opening up vast new hunting grounds for Dönitz' boats. January 1942 brought the "Paukenschlag" (Roll of Drums), the second "Happy Times". The five type IX boats that reached the US shore in January found the coast still lit at night and convoys non-existent. For the next four months, until an effective convoy system was established on the East Coast, the U-boats had perhaps their easiest pickings of the war. But, ultimately, the range of operations had to bring them to an end. Even though some success was achieved in the Caribbean after the Atlantic Coast dried up, Dönitz knew that neither operations there or around Gibraltar were going to win the Tonnageschlacht. A German study in May 1942 established that some 700,000 GRT had to be sunk monthly to strangle England. Figuring he could count on the Luftwaffe and surface raiders to account for 150,000 GRT, the remainder had to be sunk by Dönitz' boats.

The 550,000 GRT requisite figure had been exceeded in both May and June 1942, but with successes off the US coast tailing off, and the success of the combined arms attack on the Murmansk convoy PQ-17 in July (23 out of 36 merchant ships sunk, 16 by U-boat) unlikely to be repeated — because of Göring's almost continual lack of co-operation and the Kriegsmarine's re-

luctance to risk surface units — Dönitz was able, in late July, to finally convince the naval staff that victory could only be achieved by total commitment of all U-boat resources to the Mid-Atlantic battleground.

For the first time, Dönitz now felt he had the tools. His U-boats returned to the convoy battles in unprecedented numbers. At the beginning of August over 350 boats were in the water and, though many of these were newly launched and still in their six month fitting out and working up period, as many as 35 were on station at a time. New pack tactics evolved to meet this happy circumstance. Two or three sweeplines of up to 12 boats were set up to work consecutively across the convoy routes from east to west, refuel from new type IXD and XIV U-tankers near Bermuda, and then sweep back. When a particularly juicy target was sighted, more than one group could converge for massed attacks.

The results once again bore out Dönitz' theories. Sinkings not only maintained the levels attained earlier in the year during the Paukenschlag, but reached in November almost 750,000 GRT. The tallies did drop to 300,000 GRT between December 1942 and February 1943, because of bad storms, but March and better weather saw them rise dramatically again. With 50 boats in action at once, it became possible to simply overwhelm the available escorts. In what was to be the last great convoy victory, 41 U-boats converged on convoys SC-122 and HX-229 for four consecutive days be-

The "Happy Times"! Here U-552 returns in glory from the Paukenschlag off the coast of America. One of the Fourth Wave boats, U-552 sank seven ships during a patrol that lasted from 7 March to 27 April 1942. The pennants that run from the periscope to the forward end of the tower represent these seven merchantmen each one noting the ship type and rated tonnage. The captain, Kapitänleutnant Topp, in his white cap accepts the cheers of the crowd while his IWO (Executive Officer) does the work of docking the boat from his post at the bridge voice pipe, his megaphone conveniently perched on the UZO (the surface torpedo aiming apparatus). The decoration of the tower with flowers or branches was a traditional German way of celebrating the end of a successful patrol. (Bundesarchiv)

One of U-103's crew applies a special decoration celebrating perhaps the ultimate honor for a U-boat captain, at least early in the war. Having claimed the sinking of 187,843 GRT of merchant shipping, Kapitänleutnant Schütze was awarded the Oakleaves to the Knight's Cross. Overclaiming was a common problem in all navies but most of Schütze's claims held up and he ended the war as the third leading U-boat ace. The crewman uses the antenna lead insulator as the center of his Iron Cross. (Bundesarchiv)

tween 16 and 20 March 1943, sinking 22 merchant ships of 146,000 GRT against the loss of one U-boat.

Victory, so it seemed, was well within the grasp of the U-boats. With sinkings of almost 600,000 GRT in March (while losing 12 U-boats), the pace needed for victory was being achieved. Up to this point, the Allies had lost over 14,000,000 GRT from all causes and had been able to replace less than half. And by this time, U-boats were being launched at the rate of five per week. Yet with dramatic suddeness, April saw the defeat of the German submarine offensive, a defeat from which there was to be no recovery. In the next major convoy battle, that for ONS-5 in early May, 13 merchant ships were sunk but so were eight U-boats. Dönitz had seen the signs of impending disaster, had warned Hitler in September 1942. There were three primary causes for this reversal each of which alone would not have been enough, but which together turned the tide of the U-boat war against the Germans.

The first and foremost reason was the Allied victory in the "Technological War". In a battle of ploys and counter-ploys that had been going on for three years, the Allies achieved victory in early 1943. Radar had been used by the Allies since 1940, when it was first fitted into Coastal Command aircraft, but at that stage it was inaccurate and unreliable. In mid 1942, a new decimetric radar of much greater accuracy and range was introduced. But here the Germans got lucky. They discovered that the French, in their pre-

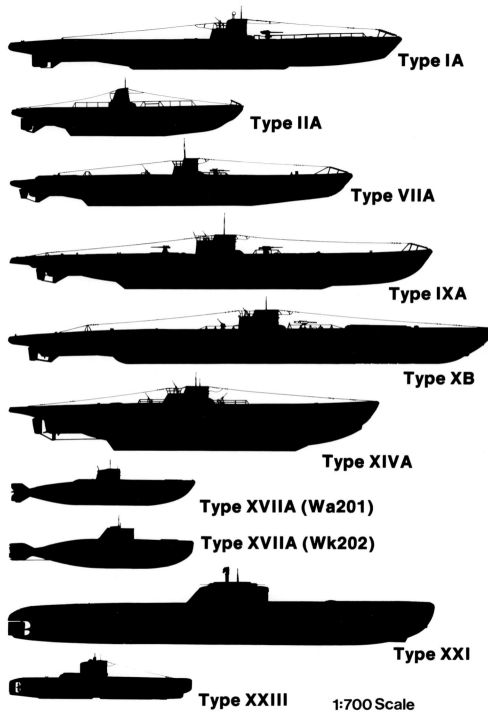

Type IA

Type IIA

Type VIIA

Type IXA

Type XB

Type XIVA

Type XVIIA (Wa201)

Type XVIIA (Wk202)

Type XXI

Type XXIII

1:700 Scale

war electronic experimentation, had developed a device called Metox which monitored decimetric wavelengths and could easily be rigged to act as a Radar Detector. With an improvised wooden, cross-braced antenna, the "Biskayakreuz," the Metox-equipped U-boat got sufficient warning to get safely submerged. This stalemate lasted until February 1943 when boats began to be attacked with no warning from the Metox. The Allies had introduced a new shorter wavelength, centimetric radar to which the Metox was not sensitive. Having been told by their scientists that centimetric radar was technologically impossible, six months passed before the first Naxos centimetric detectors were available for use and a year before they were available in quantity.

A number of other technical achievements supplemented the effectiveness of the new radar. Among them were the Leigh Light, an extremely powerful airborne searchlight; the perfection of HF/DF techniques (Huff Duff-High Frequency Direction Finding) allowing escorts to zero in on even short radio transmissions; the Hedgehog depth bomb system that shot its charges out in front of the attacking escort allowing it to hold Asdic contact; plus a stream of new ideas and refinements as the war progressed.

A second factor was the sudden increase in convoy escorts in early 1943, both airborne and surface. The "Air Gap", that area of the Atlantic not covered by air patrol, had been gradually shrinking since the war began. New bases in Iceland and the Azores helped to shrink the 'Gap' during 1942, but the sudden increase in long-range patrol planes (from 6 to 60 between January and February 1943) and the introduction of Escort Carriers on the convoy routes allowed continual air coverage all the way across the Atlantic. The importance of this cannot be overemphasized, as 46% of U-boat sinkings were by aircraft.

Likewise, in early 1943 there was a dramatic increase in the number of surface escorts available to the Allies. This was in part because war-time construction was coming into service and in part because a large number of escorts that had been pulled off convoy duty to protect the Torch landings were released. Sufficient escorts were now available so that not only could there be as many as 12 escorts per convoy but more importantly independent Escort Groups of three to five ships could be established. Since it took 2 or 3 ships to effectively attack a submerged U-boat, it was no longer necessary to weaken the convoy's defense against the remainder of the pack. Now the independent Escort Group could chase down the boat with improved techniques and the Hedgehog, with a greater chance of sinking the submarine.

But, thirdly, even without improved defensive capability the Allies would not have been defeated in the Battle of the Atlantic. Dönitz grossly underestimated the ability of the US to build ships. The figure of 700,000 GRT Allied merchant shipping sunk per month, the figure that would bring victory in the Tonnageschlacht was based on the estimation that Britain and the US together would launch in 1943 less than 8,000,000 GRT of new merchant shipping. In actuality, the launchings from US yards alone were almost double that. By July 1943, new tonnage launched surpassed all wartime losses to that point. In order to keep pace with this new construction, the U-boats would have had to double their sinkings at a time when their very ability to survive in the open sea was in question.

On one of the rare sunny days in the Far North, a Bv 138C of SAGr 130 refuels from a 11.U-Flottille boat. This meeting is probably taking place off the coast of Spitsbergen, whose fiords and bays were the haunt of U-boats throughout the war. The White over Green Splinter camouflage on the seaplane indicates the Arctic setting. This was the only theater in which Luftwaffe-Kriegsmarine co-operation was effective. (Bundesarchiv)

The defeat, when it came, was as total as it was sudden. After having sunk 97 Allied ships in the first three weeks of March, against the loss of 7 U-boats, the presence of increasing numbers of escorts forced the U-boats more and more to remain submerged and to approach convoys with greater caution. Merchant sinkings in April dropped to half of the previous months figures. "Black May" 1943 turned the tide. In that month, merchant sinkings continued to decline, but U-boat losses almost tripled from 15 to 41, (including six in one terrible night), a full 25% of operational strength. In what was to become a typical encounter, the "Elbe 2" patrol line of 11 boats converged on convoy SC-129 on 11 May, but so did Cdr. MacIntyre's Escort Group B-2, aided by U-504's homing signal. For the next three nights, all U-boat attacks were turned back by the aggressive defense of Cdr. MacIntyre, aided on the last night by the Escort Carrier HMS Biter. By the time the attack was called off on the 14th, one U-boat had been sunk and no merchant ships. On 24 May 1943, Dönitz was forced to admit defeat and recall all but a token number of boats from the Atlantic.

Against these Allied advantages, the Germans tried numerous tactical and technological responses with varying success. In reaction to strengthened defences in the North Atlantic, U-boats were sent to other waters in hopes of finding areas less well protected. Unfortunately, not only were there fewer escorts, there were also fewer targets and successes were limited.

In an attempt to counter the RAF offensive in the Bay of Biscay, Dönitz was inspired by the success of U-333 in staying on the surface and shooting down an attacking Wellington in March. He immediately ordered the modification of certain U-boats as "aircraft traps" designed to carry heavy flak armament, and to act as escort for groups of surfaced boats. The importance of being able to cross the Bay of Biscay on the surface was tremendous, as submerged crossings were slow, wasteful of supplies and hard on boats and men. Not only did being forced to cross the Bay submerged shorten by as much as half the patrol time of a U-boat, but in type VII and IX boats such primarily submerged operations led to a decline in crew morale and efficiency that was disastrous. This decline was directly caused by the fact that these boats were not really submarines in the true sense but "submersible torpedo boats" designed to work on the surface nearly all the time. In submerged operation they rapidly became hot and acquired the odor of decaying garbage. And even with this, safety was only increased, not assured, as out of every 12 hours at least two had to be spent on the surface recharging batteries.

Obviously, any solution that could keep the boats up on the surface deserved a try. The first "aircraft trap", U-441, was available in late May armed with two 2cm Flakvierlinge and a single 3.7cm mount. The potency of this flak armament surprised the RAF, almost two months passing before effective counter-measures once again turned the tables. But on the first two days of August, four U-boats in the Bay were sunk on the surface despite the beefed-up anti-aircraft protection. On 2 August 1943, Dönitz again had to admit defeat and prohibit surface crossings of the Bay of Biscay.

In a further effort to offset the Allied advantage, a number of new technological innovations were introduced. Two new torpedoes came into service, the T5 Zaunkönig acoustical torpedo which homed onto propeller noise and the FAT (Flachenabsuchender torpedo) designed to zig-zag so as to increase the chances of hitting targets in tightly packed convoys with less requirement for careful aim. Additionally, the first schnorkel-fitted boats became available in August. The schnorkel was a Dutch invention, an extendible breathing tube which allowed a U-boat's diesels to be run under water. The effect was to allow for unlimited submerged endurance. The schnorkel was hardly without problems, among them the nasty habit of plugging up in all but the calmest seas which could empty a boat of oxygen, placing an effective limit of 6 knots on a schnorkeling U-boat. But when it and the Naxos centimetric radar detector became available, Dönitz felt he

could send his boats back out again with better chance of survival. By early September, U-boats were back in the Atlantic in number again.

The first two big convoy battles of the new offensive were typical of how conditions were to be in an ocean turned hostile. In the first, 19 boats attacked two convoys between 19 and 23 September, sinking 6 merchant ships and 3 escorts against the loss of 1 U-boat. In the next, 18 U-boats attacked, sank one escort and lost 3 of their own. In order to sink the merchant ships, U-boats now had to take on and beat the escorts, a questionable proposition at best. With losses continuing at a steady rate, the decision was made to go ahead with mass production of the only real solution to Dönitz' problem, the "Elektroboot" — the first true submarine. Developed out of the Walter experimental boats, the type XXI and XXIII Electric designs had the necessary characteristics to turn the Battle of the Atlantic around, but they were still at least a year off. During that year, the U-boat had to somehow keep the pressure on, try to delay the invasion that everyone knew was coming.

By the beginning of 1944, more U-boats were being sunk than merchant ships, necessitating the cessation of all pack attacks. But while this brought losses down, merchant sinkings dropped to four in May. From then on the U-boats and the escorts played a cat and mouse game. Every time the U-boats surfaced, successes went up and so did losses (44 U-boats in August), when the U-boats submerged again successes plummeted (1 merchant sinking in October). The loss of the French Atlantic Ports in August only further complicated German problems.

The first type XXIII boats were ready, after understandable teething troubles, in February 1945. Eight type XXIII boats actually took part in operations with some success (more significantly, no losses), but were limited in their potential by their small size and armament of only two torpedos. The larger and more dangerous type XXIs were slower in coming, only two leaving on operational patrol before the end of the war. Both easily evaded Hunter-Killer groups and a mock attack carried out by U-2511 under Kptlt. Adalbert Schnee against HMS Norfolk before the cessation of hostilities showed that the new tactics worked out by Dönitz for his new boats might well have tipped the balance back in Germany's favor.

Dönitz' new tactics were designed to take maximum advantage of the type XXIs revolutionary abilities. Faster underwater than on the surface, they were designed to schnorkel at night and run on batteries during the day, spending the entire patrol submerged. Fitted with new hydrophones of extreme sensitivity and an echo chamber that allowed multiple targets to be identified and tracked underwater, attacks were to be made from a depth of 150 feet without even coming to periscope depth. Torpedo armament also reflected the new tactics, both the magnetic and accoustic torpedoes were improved and made immune to decoys, and a new model was introduced that would alter to a designated course after launch.

In spite of the excellence of the new boats and the ingenuity of the tactics, even Dönitz knew it was too late. When the two new type XXI boats left on patrol, it was just a matter of going through the motions. Before they sailed, Dönitz gave the two captains specific instructions not to sink any shipping before reaching their patrol areas. With the Allied armies slicing through their homeland, these boats could no longer effect the outcome of events.

Type I

Type IA (2)*

The type I boats were the first designed, but were neither the first ordered, nor the first in the water. They were, in fact, designated U-25 and U-26. Their design was based on the Turkish Gür, which was built in Spain from designs developed at the Dutch-based, German-owned, Submarine Development Bureau. At 860 tons, the type I boats were one third smaller than developments in other countries of fleet-type, ocean-going submarines. Nevertheless, Dönitz staff found them to be unhandy, they were poor sea boats and sluggish in maneuver. Rather than proceed with more boats of similar size and characteristics, it was decided to concentrate on the smaller type VII and larger type IX boats to carry the brunt of the U-boat War.

The type I's had been relegated to a training role before the outbreak of war, but Dönitz was so short of operational boats in 1939 that U-25 and U-26 were pressed back into service. Both were on operational patrol when sunk in mid-1940.

*This number following a type designation indicates total built.

Seen here in the late pre-war color scheme of Medium Grey with a large White numeral on the tower, U-26 was the second and last type I boat. The bulge in the deck casing in front of the tower was a gun platform, similar to that which became characteristic of the later type VIIs. Except for that bulge, the type Is looked very similar to the type IX design which evolved from them.

Type IA

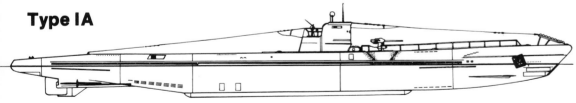

Just painted up in a fierce scheme, U-25 is ready for war. The sharkmouth and skull emblems were only carried for the first patrol of the war, being replaced by the more familiar red-capped mushroom. Noticeable is the bulge for the gun platform and the magnetic compass housing which projects in front of the tower. Recent modifications to the tower include the extension of the flange around the edge to act as a wind deflector and the addition of a new one around the center as a spray deflector. Extending above the tower is the FPR, the direction finding loop. The seaman in the foreground is in typical early deck gear. He is wearing standard U-boat leather pants with his Royal Blue peacoat over and a scarf tucked in against the cold. Only the early style naval cap which was quickly replaced by a Blue feldmütze, indicates the date of his costume. The cap band is embroidered with the title. 2. U-bootsflottille (2nd Submarine Flotilla). (Bundesarchiv)

Type II

Type IIA (6), Type IIB (20); Type IIC (8); Type IID (16)

Nicknamed "Dugout Canoes" by their German crews, the type II boats were so called because of their small size and terrible surface stability. The type IIAs weighed in at 250 tons, so light and small that they barely had enough range to adequately perform as coastal boats. They were the first Reichsmarine U-boats to be ordered and launched. The 24 boats for which parts were secretly ordered in early 1934 were all type IIA's and B's.

The type design was a direct descendant of the WWI UBII class of 1915, a fairly successful coastal type, and the Finnish-built Vesikko of 1933. Each of the succeeding sub-types after the type IIA was an attempt to increase the usefulness of the type by increasing the length to improve stability, and adding to the saddle tanks to increase operational radius. Neither modification was wholly successful.

The type II boats, from the beginning, were of only marginal usefulness in Dönitz' plans. He intended them to be used exclusively as training vessels. Yet, as was the case with the type Is, the suddenness of the onset of war and the small size of the U-boat fleet forced Dönitz to use most of the type II's operationally. They were quickly found to be totally unsuited for anti-shipping operations, and were primarily used during 1940 and early 1941 as minelayers. The type IIDs, which came into service in early 1941, had triple the range of the IIAs and were intended for offensive patrols. But even they were found to be too small to carry sufficient torpedoes and too unhandy on the surface to be very useful. In June 1941 all type IIs were withdrawn from the Atlantic and were assigned to the Baltic to be used for training with occasional sorties against Russian coastal shipping.

The most successful operational theater of the type IIs was, however, just being opened up. In late summer 1941, six type IIB boats (U-9, U-18, U-19, U-20, U-23, U-24) were transported by rail to Constantia, Rumania for use against the Russian naval re-supply of Sevastopol. These six boats were to operate with considerable success in the Black Sea until late 1944, only one being lost to enemy action. Most type II boats, because of their Baltic location and training duties, survived the war to be scuttled or surrendered in 1945.

The type IIBs were virtually indistinguishable from the As, the primary differences being internal. Visible at the bow of these boats is the net cutter, which was to characterize all but the last U-boat designs. Also noticeable are the projecting navigation lights on the towers, these were recessed on all later boats. The four boats visible, U-10, U-9, U-11 and U-7 (Left to Right), were part of the first permanent Flotilla, the 1. U-Flottile (Flottille Weddigen), a training unit based at Kiel.

The first of many, U-1, a type IIA boat, is seen here in an early propaganda shot. Flying overhead is a staffel of Luftwaffe He 60Cs. This early appearance of Air-Sea co-operation was for show only. In fact, lack of this co-operation was to be a major factor in the failure of the U-boat offensive. U-1 was the first German U-boat since the Versailles treaty. The product of secret design and construction, it was commissioned just 12 days after its existence was legitimized by the Anglo-German Naval Agreement. As originally designed, it carried the FPR externally at the front of the bridge, but this was found to be a vulnerable position.

U-3, another of the six type IIAs, shows the cleanness of its lines. It also shows off its early pre-war paint scheme, overall Light Grey with a large Black numeral on the tower side and the ship's full designation carried on a metal plate on either side of the bow. This plate was maintained after the switch to the late pre-war colors in 1938, but was dropped at the outbreak of war. The photo can be dated as having been taken during 1935, as U-3 still flies the Reichsmarine flag, which was replaced by the Kriegsmarine ensign late that year.

Type IIA

Type IIB

Type IIC

Type IID

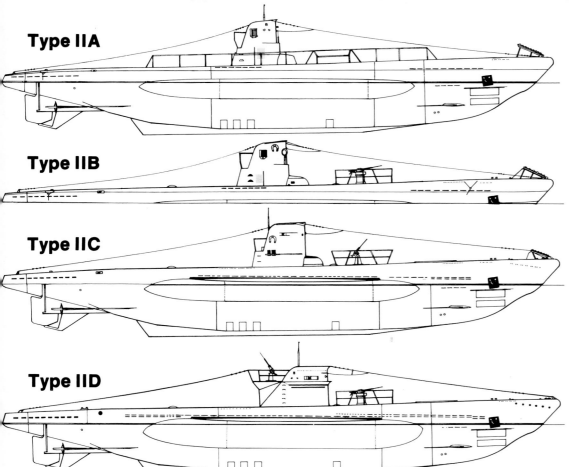

This unidentified type IIC boat shows the increased free-flooding holes that distinguished it from its predecessors. Also the Cs were the first designed to carry deck armament, a 2cm Flak (officially a 2cm C/30 in LC30). Some of these boats were used operationally for a time, though their limitations severely restricted their usefulness. That this is one that achieved such status can be ascertained by the fact that it carries an individual boat emblem, in this case, a leaping devil holding a cocked hat. (Bundesarchiv)

Coming into service in early 1941, the type IIDs, because of their extended range, were intended as fully operational boats. But they came too late. With sufficient range to operate off the coast of England, they might have succeeded two years earlier. But with total Allied air superiority in that area, they now were forced to play the role of ocean-going boats, for which they were totally unsuited. This boat, U-141, under Oberleutnant zur See Schüler, attacked two convoys in June 1941, sinking two merchant ships, before being withdrawn to the Baltic as a training boat. She carries a typical mid-war camouflage of Light and Dark Grey.

The first of Dönitz' Wolfpack boats, the type VIIAs were immediately popular with their crews, being excellent sea boats. U-30 under Kapitänleutnant Lemp is seen entering Lorient in late June 1940, the first boat to enter one of the newly captured French ports. U-30 was notorious for another "first", being the boat that sank the British liner Athenia on 3 September 1939, the first U-boat victim of the war. Visible before the bridge is the bulge in the deck casing for the 8.8cm gun platform that was to be an identifying characteristic of all type VIIs, as well as the curve of the saddle tanks breaking the waterline behind the bridge. This boat is identifiable as an A by the above water aft torpedo tube, visible through the exhaust smoke.

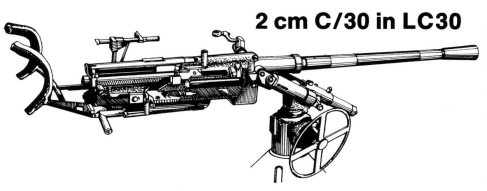

2 cm C/30 in LC30

U-30 is again seen in the background, behind UA. Like the later VIIBs, the A series suffered from inadequate ventilation, and like them, most VIIAs had an external duct added to the tower side, visible curving under the Flak platform, the "Wintergarten". UA, not looking much like any other German design, was completing construction as the Turkish "Batiray" at the Germania Werft when war broke out. Taken over by the Kriegsmarine, it was similar internally and in size to the later type IXD, but had such atypical external features as the raised gun platform in front of the bridge and enclosed conning position at its top. The bulges at the sides were for mine stowage. (Bundesarchiv)

A good clean view of a type VIIB as built, U-45 is seen here in the late pre-war Dark Grey. The main visual differences from the previous sub-type were the relocation of the aft torpedo tube, now underwater, and the increase by half of the saddle tanks causing a change in the pattern of free-flooding holes along the side of the deck casing. U-45 had the dubious distinction of being one of the first boats lost, sinking in October 1939. (Bundesarchiv)

Type VII

Type VIIA (10); Type VIIB (24); Type VIIC (over 600); Type VIID (6); Type VIIE (project); Type VIIF (4)

In the type VIIs, particularly the main VIIC sub-type, Dönitz had found the boat he was looking for. In it he found a medium-size (626 ton), highly maneuverable, excellent sea-boat that had the additional advantage of being cheaper and smaller than rival projects, which meant that more could be built within naval budget and within the tonnage limits of the Anglo-German Naval Agreement.

The design of the type VIIA was derived directly from that of the German-designed, Finnish "Vetehinen" of 1931. That design, in turn, grew out of the First World War UBIII class submarines of 516 tons, among the most successful boats of that period. The A sub-type had most characteristics in common with the rest of the type VIIs, particularly the external saddle tanks amidship for stowage of fuel oil which gave the type its readily identifiable bulge at the waterline. The single stern torpedo tube on the VIIAs was carried above the waterline, distinguishing them from the rest of the series.

The B sub-type was a minor revision of the A. The hull was lengthened by seven feet and the saddle tanks increased in capacity to improve the operational radius of the boats by half. More powerful diesels gave the VIIBs greater surface speed. The chief failing of the design to this point was that they suffered from inadequate and poorly positioned ventilation intakes. As they were refitted during the course of the war, external ventilation ducting was added to most of the boats to alleviate the problem. This is the only recognition feature which distinguished Bs from the later VIICs.

The type VIIC was to be the most produced single design in submarine history. Over 600 were completed and many more approached completion at war's end, even though by then they were hopelessly obsolete. But at the time of its introduction the type VIIC was a potent, maneuverable, sea worthy craft, large enough to be able to roam the Atlantic, yet small enough to be easy to build. It was Dönitz' boat. With the outbreak of war, it was the type VIIC that was standardized as the boat on which the emergency construction plans would concentrate. During the war, numerous internal changes brought sub- sub-types into being, most notably the type VIIC/41 which had a strengthened pressure hull allowing dives of an extra 25m, to a depth of 125m (though in emergencies, more than double that depth was known to have been achieved).The type VIIC/42 had improved lightweight die-

Most of the early U-boat Aces achieved their fame and success at the helm of type VIIBs. Perhaps the most famous was Kapitänleutnant Gunther Prien, the "Bull of Scapa Flow". It was Prien and his U-47 that slipped into Scapa Flow on the night of 13-14 October 1939 and sank the battleship HMS Royal Oak. Besides this extraordinary single exploit, Prien was credited with the first "official" U-boat victory on 5 September (not counting Lemp's sinking of the Athenia which the Kriegsmarine denied) and was a leading Ace until U-47 was lost with all hands on 8 March 1941. (Top Right) U-47 is seen on its triumphant return to Kiel. Note the "Snorting Bull", Prien's personal insignia, on the tower, and the small spray deflector that has been added to that structure. (Center Right) Prien being greeted by Grossadmiral Raeder. On this day, Dönitz was promoted to Konteradmiral and two days hence, Prien became the first U-boat commander to receive the Ritterkreuz. (Right) On the next voyage, U-47, still bound by prize rules, receives the papers of a Portuguese steamer for verification of neutral status and non-contraband cargo. It was not until the end of the year that unrestricted U-boat war was allowed even close to the British Isles. A standard modification of many early-war type VIIs were the anti-spray flaps on either side of the gun position. As the deck gun became less important as the war progressed, these were seen less frequently.

sels. Neither of these alterations caused any visible external difference in the basic type. German sources refer to other sub-sub-types (types VIIC/42A, 42B and 43), but it is impossible to tell if such boats ever existed. A number of major external changes in the sub-type were built into new boats, or retrofitted into many older ones, during its production run without designation changes. The most notable of these changes was the proliferation of anti-aircraft armament with the accompanying enlargement of the "Wintergarten", the open platform at the aft end of the bridge. Less noticeable were such additions as the disposition of water tight containers for inflatable life rafts , or the fitting of the new echo chamber (Balkon Gerät) under the bow.

The type VIID was a lengthened C with the extra space used behind the bridge for five free-flooding containers for three mines each. The extra length increased range but reduced speed.

The type VIIE was a project to be built around a super-lightweight V-type diesel, but as the engine never reached operational reliability, the project was dropped.

The type VIIF, last of the VIIs, was similar to the D in that it had an additional hull section added after the bridge, but carried spare torpedoes instead of mines. As many as 25 torpedoes could be carried for transfer to other U-boats, extending endurance. But torpedo transfer on the high seas was an operation that trapped two boats on the surface for long periods of time, and with improving Allied air patrol during 1943-1944, these boats became a liability.

U-99, another VIIB, approaches the pier on 10 November 1940, showing four victory flags, two of them miniature Royal Navy White Ensigns. The boat was that of Kapitänleutnant Otto Kretschmer, the leading U-boat ace of the war, and the pennants celebrated his victory in a seven-hour running battle with two British auxiliary cruisers. Kretschmer became the first U-boat commander to receive the Swords and Oakleaves to the Knight's Cross. The boat has received standard mid-war modifications while retaining the anti-spray flaps for the deck gun. These include the enlarged wind and spray deflectors on the tower, and the enlarged "Wintergarten," to which the 2cm Flak has been moved from the after deck.

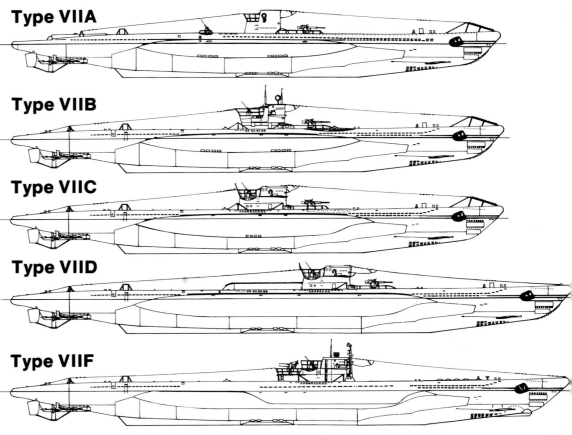

Type VIIA

Type VIIB

Type VIIC

Type VIID

Type VIIF

Insignia could pop up in a number of different places, sometimes changing boats in the process. Often they were associated with individuals as well as boats, for example, the famous "Black Cat Times Three". The symbol was originally that of U-48, commanded by Kapitänleutnant Herbert Schultze. (Above Left) U-48, a type VIIB, was the most successful U-boat of the war, at this stage already halfway to its total of over 300,000 GRT, as is shown by the large White numbers on the tower along with the boat's insignia, made fancier with a White face, and Schultze's personal emblem, the "White Witch". While the tonnage figure, as was the case with the photo on page 8, is just a temporary marking, a famous commander could add his emblem to that of the boat when taking over an already famous boat. (Below Left) Schultze himself, cradling a bouquet, was the fifth leading Ace of the war. His cap is adorned with a pin fashioned with his boat's symbol, a not uncommon practice. (Bundesarchiv) (Above) Supervising the docking is U-48's IWO, Oberleutnant zur See Suhren, seen here wearing an army-style rubberized motoring coat and sporting a similar pin on his cap. Suhren later commanded U-564, taking the symbol with him. He was one of only 29 U-boat commanders to win the late war decoration, the "U-boots-kriegsabzeichen mit Brillanten" (U-boat War Badge with Diamonds). (Bundesarchiv) (Below) A crewman of U-564 (type VIIC) takes down his boat's victory pennants showing claims for three freighters and three tankers, each carrying the boat's adopted emblem. (Bundesarchiv)

(Above Left) U-101 is seen beginning the passage across the Bay of Biscay on its way to another war patrol. It is in typical mid-war type VIIB configuration. Similar to the type VIIAs, a ventilation duct has been added to the tower side, though in this case only partially up the side. (Bundesarchiv)

(Below Left) U-83 entering the harbor at La Spezia, Italy in February 1942 shows yet another aspect. The additional ventilation ducting has been run up the center of the tower, not visible here, and the Wintergarten has been further enlarged, with the tower side extended for support. While this is also a type VIIB, it has many differences from the other two on this page which also differ from each other. This can in part be explained by the fact that they came from three different yards, each of which could interpret directives in its own way. Of particular interest is the minor difference in pattern of free-flooding holes in the hull casing, U-83 having an additional set of holes under the gun platform that were intended to further increase diving speed. (Bundesarchiv)

(Above) Another mid-war VIIB, U-73 is seen entering Lorient in April 1941, painted in an overall Dark Grey camouflage scheme. This boat also has the added ventilation ducting of the more normal pattern, extending up the side of the bridge. Like a number of other U-boats, U-73 was adopted by a German city, in this case Duisburg, carrying its crest on the tower. (Bundesarchiv)

(Below) A close-up of the bridge of U-73 taken at the same time. Kapitänleutnant Rosenbaum salutes in response to the reception. Under his command a year later, U-73 sank the British Aircraft Carrier HMS Eagle. Note the variety of dress worn by the officers, including a British Battle Blouse on the left. Note also the periscope housing with its protective rails. (Bundesarchiv)

(Left) Looking down onto the tower of a type VIIB, U-86, from the same builder as U-83, Flenderwerft of Lubeck. From front to back, the items visible are the 2cm Flak C/30 in LC 30/37, the added central ventilation duct, the attack periscope housing with periscope fully retracted, the main compass housing, the UZO and the "sky" periscope housing. At the tower's front, to the left of the central group, is the engineroom telegraph indicator, above which is a compass repeater. To the right the voice pipe and housing for the retracted FPR. Note also the steps along the tower sides for the lookouts. (Bundesarchiv)

Two more views of U-86's tower taken at different times. (Above) The leather garb of everyone in view indicates cold weather. The IWO is just visible in the upper right while one of the junior leutnants is waiting at the UZO. The Unterwasserzieloptik (UZO) was the main attack position before Allied air supremacy forced the U-boats to remain submerged. It was the surface torpedo aiming device, linked directly to the attack computer in the tower. Here it is shown with night binoculars attached. (Bundesarchiv) (Below) In a slightly warmer time, the UZO has the binoculars removed, but the binocular support still attached. That too could be removed, leaving a two-pin open sight aiming device. (Bundesarchiv)

Torpedoes

The Kriegsmarine used two basic torpedoes, which were fitted with a variety of guidance and detonation systems. The G7a was a Whitehead-type, compressed air driven, 21 inch torpedo of six km range at 44 knots. It was a fast and reliable torpedo, but left a telltale trail of bubbles, a grave disadvantage. Immediately prior to the war, the Germans introduced a new model, the G7e (meaning type G, ie. seventh model; 7 meters long; electric drive) Over the same six km it could only reach a maximum of 30 kts but it left no trail, which made it extremely popular with U-boatmen.

At the outbreak of war, German torpedoes were either fitted with a standard contact fuse or a newly invented magnetic detonator of great promise. The chief advantage of the magnetic trigger was that the torpedo could be set to run deeper to be set off under a ship by its magnetic field. While many an Allied merchant vessel limped home with a hole punched in its side by a contact torpedo, the force of the magnetic torpedo's explosion under the keel was almost always enough to "break the back" of any ship, ensuring its sinking. However, the magnetic fuse was erratic in operation and was constantly being taken out of service for improvement. It was not considered totally reliable and put into mass production until late 1944.

Two new torpedo variants were introduced in 1943 in response to worsening conditions for U-boats. Both required less careful aiming and were therefore faster to fire, increasing a U-boat's chance of survival. The T5 "Zaunkönig" acoustic torpedo was guided to the loudest sound in the water, which was hopefully the propellor noise of a target. The T5 was considered primarily an anti-escort weapon, as they had more powerful, louder engines than any other ships in the area. The second torpedo type, the Fat (Flachenabsuchender torpedo - shallow searching torpedo) was specifically an anti-convoy device. It was designed to run straight for a set distance and begin a random pattern of zig-zags. The theory, which proved to be correct, was that once among the crowded rows of a convoy, sooner or later it would hit something.

While the Fat (sometimes referred to as Lut) was immediately successful, the T5 proved disappointing. British Intelligence knew of the existence of the acoustic torpedo before it came into service and had a response ready. Almost as soon as it was introduced, convoy escorts were fitted with "Foxers" (Decoys) which were noise-making devices, louder than the ship itself, which were trailed behind. And perhaps most disastrously, occasionally the torpedo would decide that the U-boat itself was the loudest noise around, reverse direction and sink the boat that launched it. Not until late 1944 were all its bugs worked out.

Thus in early 1945 the new Elektroboot were being sent out with an unequalled arsenal of torpedoes. Not only did they carry the now perfected acoustic and magnetic torpedoes, but they had a new model which could be set to change to and hold any course desired. It is, perhaps, most fortunate for the Allies that this weapon was never fully brought to bear.

(Above Left) The ruling triumvirate of U-boat operations for most of the war. In the center, Grossadmiral Dönitz, Befehlshaber der U-boote (BdU), on the right, Konteradmiral Eberhard Godt, called "The Godfather", Chef der Operationsabteilung (Oa) and on the left, Kapitänleutnant Adalbert Schnee, Ia of Oa. This photo was taken during 1943 when U-boat HQ (also called BdU) had been moved to Hotel am Steinplatz, Charlottenburg - Berlin.

(Above) Schnee at his previous employment, that of captain of U-201. He had run up a total of 23 ships sunk of over 95,000 GRT before his transfer to BdU in late 1941. He is seen here posing at the attack periscope. His normal attack station was in the tower. (Bundesarchiv)

The same side of the control room seen from a different angle showing the two planesmen at their stations, controling the depth of the boat by means of the fore and aft diving planes. The cramped interior of a U-boat can be seen. (Bundesarchiv)

The Torpedo Mate looks after his "eels". Every four or five days, the ready torpedoes had to be withdrawn from the tubes for maintenance, a most unpleasant chore. With five tubes on a type VII boat, this was usually done one per day to keep as many ready as possible. The "eel" being worked on here is a G7e. This shot of the forward torpedo room of a type VII shows three of the four tubes, the rail on which torpedoes are loaded. Of interest is the name, it appears to be Rozmarie, given to upper right tube. (Bundesarchiv)

Torpedo transfer on the high seas, here U-154 supplies a spare "eel" to U-564. As can be readily seen, such operations required large numbers on deck, the erection of winches and hoists and the opening of most hatches, an extremely vulnerable condition. Neither boat would be able to dive if discovered by air or sea search. Such scenes, of necessity, became less and less common as the war proceeded.

Looking down on the deck gun of a type VII boat, the naval mount of the 8.8. This gun was a naval development, designated 8.8cm Schiffskanone C/35 in Unterseebootslafette C/35 (or "8.8cm Sk C/35 in Ubts LC/35" for short). It was in no way related to the Army's 8.8cm Flak or Pak guns, not even the ammunition being interchangeable. (Bundesarchiv)

The deck gun of U-552, type VIIC, is shown fully manned. Aimer and layer are at their stations, in their padded braces, while the loader stands behind them. These three men could, if conditions required, be strapped into their positions, while the three ammunition ratings could not and therefore wear life jackets even in calm seas. Note the tompion has been removed and placed on its storage hole on the gun's pedestal. Note also the "hammer" of the hydrophone visible near the bow. These were fitted to new boats, and retrofitted to old, from mid-war on. (Bundesarchiv)

Another view of the deck gun of an unidentified type VII. The gun had identical laying and aiming controls on either side so that ammunition could be passed directly to the gun from the hatch no matter its orientation without obstructing the gunners' view. But the gun only had a single set of sighting instruments which had to be switched from side to side if the gunners changed position. Each position also had padded chest braces to help the gunners keep steady aim in rough seas. Note the watertight muzzle plug (tompion) in place, attached to the gun by a line seen wound around the barrel. (Bundesarchiv)

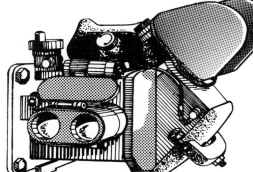

8.8 cm
Gun Sights

Three views of the type VII tower, showing detail and the evolution of features. (Above) U-706, type VIIC is seen on a shakedown cruise. The UZO, against which a Naval official is leaning, is without the binocular support attachment. A ledge has been added around the front of the tower to protect the instruments there from weather. The FPR (Funkpeilrahmen-DF Loop) is seen here fully extended. Note also the wooden strips applied to the inside walls of the tower to protect lookouts from freezing to metal surfaces. (Bundesarchiv) (Right) The tower of U-552 showing the minimal three crewmen who had to be up top when the boat was surfaced, two lookouts and a watch officer. The C series, benefiting from prior experience, now has the extra ventilation built in, the intake grating visible on the left. Midwar additions found on many U-boats were up to four MG34s, one of which can be seen here. They were intended as anti-aircraft weapons, though they were not successful at much more than boosting morale. (Bundesarchiv) (Far Right) The crew of U-571 (type VIIC) watches a merchantman take its final plunge. This boat has the most common type of VIIC ventilation pattern, exhausting through grated vents at the after edge of the tower. (Bundesarchiv)

Pulling into harbor at Bergen, Norway, a type VIIC of the 11. U-Flottille shows a good example of arctic camouflage, Light Grey hull and White tower. In common with most boats of the 11. U-Flottille, it carries two insignia, it's own on the centerline and the flotilla's to the side. A typical mid-war boat, it was built with the enlarged Wintergarten and spray and wind deflectors, without the cable cutter. (Bundesarchiv)

Another view of a typical mid-war type VIIC, in this case U-203. Another boat that carried two insignia, it had the coat of arms of the city of Essen on the tower front, barely visible here, and Kapitänleutnant Mützelburg's personal insignia, the Sea Turtle, on the tower side. Seen here entering Brest harbor on 3 April 1943, it has at least three MG34s installed on the bridge, and for the occasion has raised its "Commander's Flagpole" from which flies the commissioning pennant. (Bundersarchiv)

A North Atlantic boat, U-565 carries a typical German camouflage. Most U-boats wore some variation on the standard overall Kriegsmarine Light or Dark Grey at sometime in their career. There were regional variations in camouflage, the most bold examples, such as this splinter style, being found on the boats that fought the Battle of the Atlantic.

Type VIIC

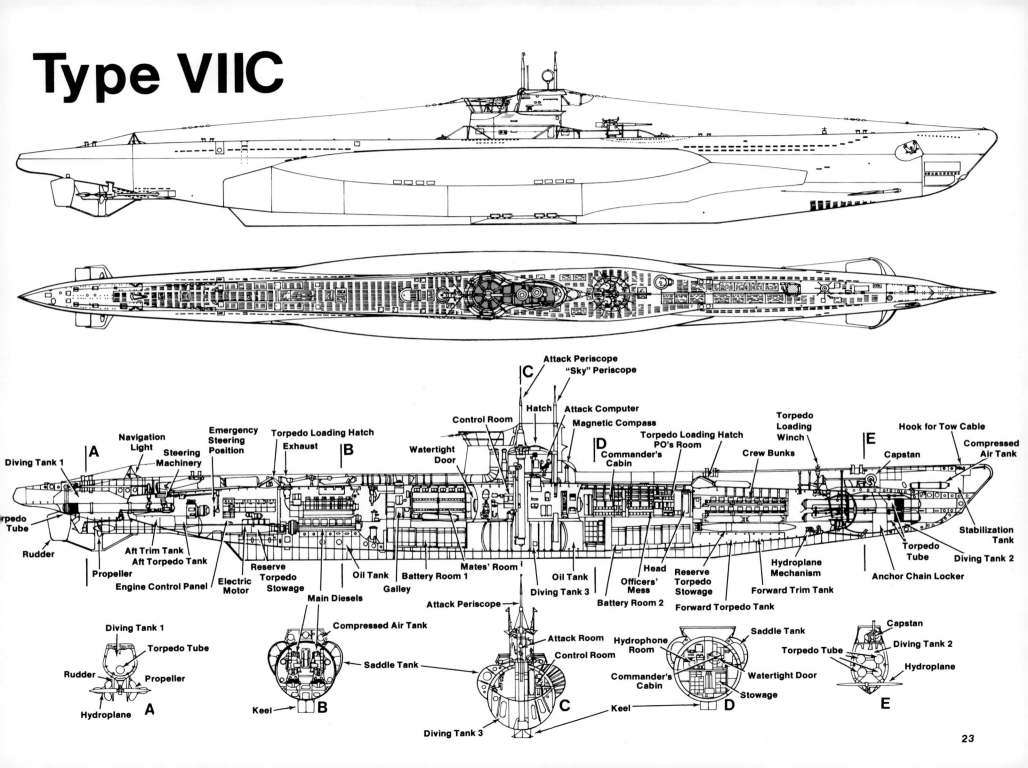

Navigation Light
Steering Machinery
Emergency Steering Position
Torpedo Loading Hatch
Exhaust
Diving Tank 1
A
B
Torpedo Tube
Rudder
Propeller
Aft Trim Tank
Aft Torpedo Tank
Engine Control Panel
Electric Motor
Reserve Torpedo Stowage
Main Diesels
Oil Tank
Galley
Battery Room 1
Compressed Air Tank
Watertight Door
Control Room
Attack Periscope
"Sky" Periscope
Hatch
Attack Computer
Magnetic Compass
Mates' Room
Commander's Cabin
Torpedo Loading Hatch
PO's Room
Diving Tank 3
Oil Tank
Head
Officers' Mess
Battery Room 2
Reserve Torpedo Stowage
Forward Torpedo Tank
Crew Bunks
Hydroplane Mechanism
Forward Trim Tank
Torpedo Loading Winch
Anchor Chain Locker
Capstan
Hook for Tow Cable
Compressed Air Tank
Stabilization Tank
Torpedo Tube
Diving Tank 2

Diving Tank 1
Torpedo Tube
Rudder
Propeller
Hydroplane
A

Saddle Tank
Keel
B

Attack Periscope
Attack Room
Control Room
Commander's Cabin
Keel
Diving Tank 3
C

Hydrophone Room
Saddle Tank
Watertight Door
Stowage
D

Capstan
Diving Tank 2
Torpedo Tube
Hydroplane
E

23

After a U-boat had completed its six month working-up period with one of the Baltic training flotillas, it was declared "Frontreif"- ready for action, and was allowed the honor of painting an insignia on the boat's tower. Nearly all boats carried some emblem, though only half were "personal" insignia, many carrying just the flotilla's emblem. (Far Left) The emblem of 7. U-Flottille, the "Bull of Scapa Flow", Gunther Prien's personal insignia that was taken over by his old flotilla after his death. (Bundesarchiv) (Left) "Laughing Sawfish" of the 9. U-Flottille, in this case carried with the city crest of Danzig on U-407. (Bundesarchiv) (Above) An unknown boat of the 11. U-Flottille based in Norway. Appropriately enough, the emblem was a bow-on view of a U-boat superimposed over a polar bear. (Bundersarchiv)

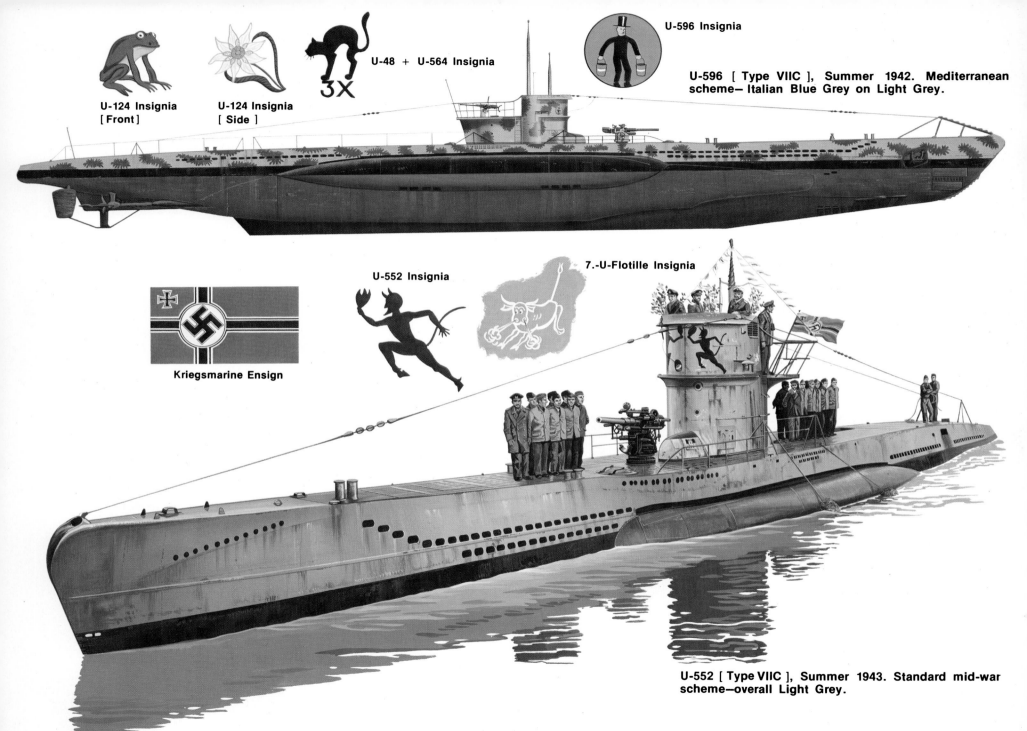

U-124 Insignia
[Front]

U-124 Insignia
[Side]

3X

U-48 + U-564 Insignia

U-596 Insignia

U-596 [Type VIIC], Summer 1942. Mediterranean scheme— Italian Blue Grey on Light Grey.

U-552 Insignia

7.-U-Flotille Insignia

Kriegsmarine Ensign

U-552 [Type VIIC], Summer 1943. Standard mid-war scheme—overall Light Grey.

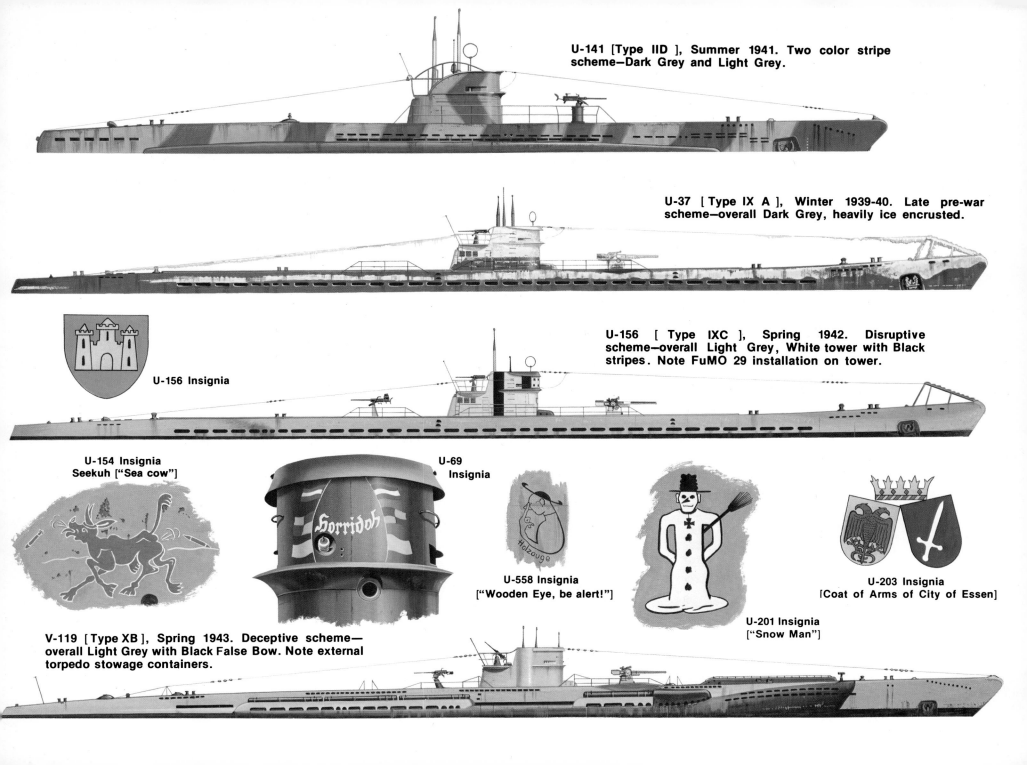

U-141 [Type IID], Summer 1941. Two color stripe scheme—Dark Grey and Light Grey.

U-37 [Type IX A], Winter 1939-40. Late pre-war scheme—overall Dark Grey, heavily ice encrusted.

U-156 [Type IXC], Spring 1942. Disruptive scheme—overall Light Grey, White tower with Black stripes. Note FuMO 29 installation on tower.

U-156 Insignia

U-154 Insignia
Seekuh ["Sea cow"]

U-69
Insignia

U-558 Insignia
["Wooden Eye, be alert!"]

U-201 Insignia
["Snow Man"]

U-203 Insignia
[Coat of Arms of City of Essen]

V-119 [Type XB], Spring 1943. Deceptive scheme—overall Light Grey with Black False Bow. Note external torpedo stowage containers.

Personal insignias varied from crude, temporary ones to very fancy examples. (Above) Celebrating its only return from patrol in its short career, U-556 displays a stick-figure knight sinking two merchant ships and a claim of 49,900 GRT sunk. (Bundesarchiv) (Above Right) A much more elaborate emblem, the German warcry "Horridoh" surrounded by signal flags, decorates the tower of U-69. The first of the VIICs, U-69 has just been commissioned and the emblem just applied. The tripod rigged above the bridge is the collapsible winch tower used on the open sea to help move torpedoes from deck stowage to the torpedo room. (Bundesarchiv) (Below Right) U-753, seen here in June 1942 at St. Nazaire carrying a skull and crossbones insignia, a popular one with U-boats, with the added motto "Noch und Noch!" which translates "still and again." (Bundesarchiv) (Below) "Wooden Eye", U-558, returns to a French port in June 1942, flying seven pennants signifying victories off the American coast, one of whose ensigns was recovered and displayed. The insignia refers to an old German folktale about a cuckolded minister with a false eye and the admonition "Holzauge sei Wach". (Wooden Eye, be alert!) This is one of the few examples of a U-boat actually carrying a life preserver in the stowage position indicating most crew's attitude toward their usefulness. (Bundesarchiv)

(Above) An elegantly camouflaged type VIIC docks in one of the French ports, riding high at the end of a patrol. Two victory pennants can be seen flying from the "Commander's Flagpole". This boat displays a standard mid-war modification, the addition of a retractable rod antenna to the port side of the tower, seen partially extended here, and the consequent housing bulge. (Bundesarchiv)

(Left) The "Wild Donkey", so named because it slipped its ways at launching, returns from the last great convoy battle, the fight for HX.229 and SC.122 in March 1943. U-338 is seen here flying five victory pennants, the uppermost being for a Coastal Command Halifax shot down during the return across the Bay of Biscay. This is one of few cases of underclaiming, as U-338 had actually sunk five merchantmen in this battle.

(Right) Being escorted through the safe waters off the French Coast, U-132 shows to good advantage the housing for the rod antenna. The installation of this antenna was occasioned by the increasing range at which U-boats worked in 1942. Sunning himself on the magnetic compass housing is Kapitänleutnant Vogelsang, one of the few U-boat commanders to incorporate Nazi heraldry into his boats insignia. (Bundesarchiv)

One of the boats that served with the 29.U-Flottille based a La Spezia, U-596 displays typical Mediterranean Camouflage. All boats that served in the Mediterranean for any length of time acquired a similar paint job of Italian Blue-Grey splotches over Kriegsmarine Light Grey. U-596 is seen here with an extended and braced Wintergarten allowing the installation of an ammunition stowage container seen in the bridge decking immediately aft of the attack periscope. (Bundesarchiv)

(Left Above & Below) U-203 is seen on two different occasions, above on its way out to the Fourth Wave of the Paukenschlag, and below on its return from its next patrol with five victories in July 1942. The above shot shows the commissioning pennant flying for this special occasion, and the boat's insignia, the coat of arms of the city of Essen. The photo below shows to good advantage the fully extended rod antenna and the method used to carry the jumper cables around the antenna housing and Wintergarten. Note the pivoting travel lock for the 2cm Flak and the recess in the deck for its stowage. Also of interest is the folding canvas "deck chair," presumably for the captain's use, in the lower right corner. (Bundesarchiv)

The Short Sunderland, the first element in the formula that defeated the U-boat. It was Allied airpower, more than any other factor, that broke the back of the U-boat offensive. Called "Müde Bienen" (Tired Bees) by the U-boatmen because they were slow and ungraceful, but they could carry a large load of depth charges and sophisticated radar arrays, eventually coming to dominate the sky over the Bay of Biscay though limited range still left a gap in air coverage in the North Atlantic.

The CAM ship with its "Catafighter" was the first attempt to close the Air Gap. The Catapult Aircraft Merchantship was conceived to combat attacks by Fw 200 Condors but was primarily employed as an anti-submarine tool. Enough CAM ships were in operation in late 1941 that one was assigned to nearly every other convoy, but the idea never was too popular with either pilots or the convoymen, and was allowed to lapse in 1942. A short-range fighter, even when armed with light bombs, is not an ideal anti-submarine aircraft, while ditching in the North Atlantic after a single four-hour patrol was hardly something to look forward to.

The Air Gap was finally closed by the introduction of extended range patrol planes, such as the V.L.R. Liberators, and "Hunter-Killer" escort groups such as seen here. Frequently built around an escort carrier, always with three or more surface escorts, these groups were not assigned to any one convoy but were free to stay with the fight as long as necessary, at times following one contact for several days. The key to this victory was the productivity of US shipyards, both the escort carrier and Evarts class destroyer escort, seen here in Royal Navy service, were of American construction.

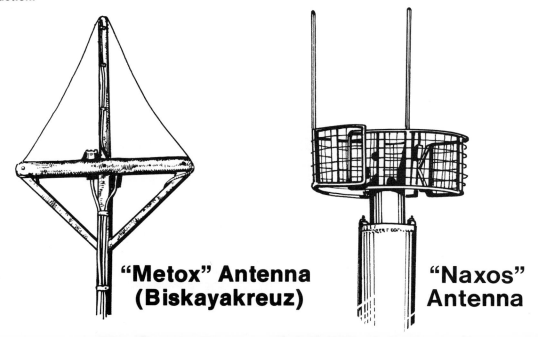

"Metox" Antenna (Biskayakreuz)

"Naxos" Antenna

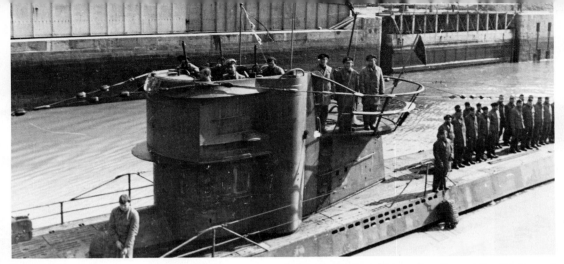

The German response to the increased Allied defense included the introduction of the Metox set with its Biskayakreuz antenna, the FuMo 29 (Funkmessortung 29) rigid radar and increased anti-aircraft armament. (Above) Introduced in 1942, the FuMo 29 array was attached to the front of the tower, a row of receiving antennae over a row of sending, in nearly all cases covered with a protective shield as seen here. In order to make a 360° search, the boat had to sail in a complete circle. Added to the short range and inaccuracy of its half-meter wavelength, this made it less than satisfactory in operation. (Bundesarchiv) (Top Right) In an attempt to contest the RAF's air offensive over the Bay of Biscay in late 1942, the Germans took U-441 in hand and modified it as seen here. Two 2cm Flakvierlinge were mounted along with a single 3.7cm Flak. Intended as a surface anti-aircraft escort, U-441 was renamed U-Flak 1, achieving some initial success. The RAF soon developed tactics that neutralized its concentrated fire power, and it was returned to duty as an attack submarine. (Right Center) Simultaneous with introduction of "Flak-traps" such as U-441, an attempt was made to strengthen the air defense of remaining U-boats. Most frequently this took the form of a second Wintergarten platform being added below and astern of the original, with a consequent increase in flak mounts. At first the increase was a simple doubling by the addition of a second 2cm Flak as is the case in this Arctic boat. (Bundesarchiv) (Bottom Right) As the war progressed, Flak defense of U-boats continued to be augmented as Wintergartens were expanded. In this shot, a typical late-war type VII configuration can be seen; two twin 2cm mounts on the upper level, a shielded 2cm Flakvierling on the lower. This additional Flak was frequently accompanied by the removal of the deck gun. (Bundesarchiv)

Type VIIC/42

U-Flak-1 (U-441)

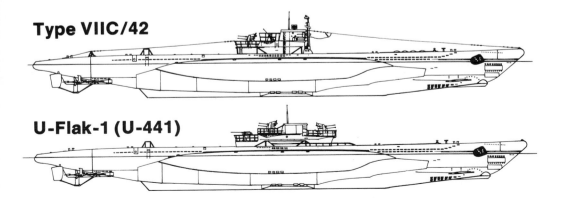

When development of centimetric radar was belatedly recommenced by Germany, a vital side benefit was the introduction of a radar detector effective in detecting the latest Allied types. Unfortunately the new detector, called Naxos, was never available in quantity, one of the lucky boats is seen here with the distinctive antenna partially extended. (Bundesarchiv)

Centimetric radar was eventually introduced into U-boat service in 1944, in the form of the FuMo 30 set with its rotating antenna seen on this boat. Like the Naxos, the radar was never available in great quantity, this boat having both the new and old (FuMo 29) antennae. On the old radar cover has been painted one of the most exclusive U-boat markings, the Olympic Rings, indicating the commander was a graduate of the Naval Academy in 1938, the year of the Berlin Games.

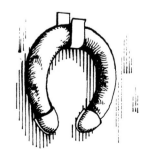

"Horseshoe" Life Preserver

Two late-war type VIIs are seen in harbor. Visible are the widened Wintergarten, the mount for the deck gun (which has been removed) and the housing for the FuMo 30 antenna on the tower side. (Bundesarchiv)

U-1009 shows the typical appearance of a type VII in 1945. Besides the extended Wintergarten, visible modifications include the schnorkel, seen retracted in its trough in the deck casing and four containers for liferafts near the bow.

Schnorkels

The schnorkel, so long associated with U-boats, was not originally a German idea. Rather, it was of Dutch origin, having been first experimentally fitted on the Royal Netherlands Navy Submarine O 21, in February 1940. The fitting was an arrangement of two periscopic pipes, one with a floating ball valve (to preclude the accidental intake of water) was the air inlet, the second was a valveless exhaust pipe. The end result was the first practical apparatus that allowed a U-boat's diesels, its main method of propulsion, to be run underwater.

With the capture of Holland in May 1940, all records of this research fell into German hands. Yet, rather than capitalize upon this stroke of luck, the Kriegsmarine made no efforts to employ or improve the schnorkel until the disastrous spring of 1943 brought the idea back into favor. But now, instead of having a new boat designed from the outset for schnorkel use, the Germans were forced to modify existing type VII and IX boats. While these boats did yeoman service between 1943 and 1945, they were constantly limited by the fact that they were not designed for continuous submerged operation.

The schnorkel with which these boats were fitted was a simple modification of the original Dutch design. The twin periscopic pipes were replaced by a single rigid tube which could, by pivoting at its base, be lowered into a well in the deck casing. Still fitted with a floating ball cutoff valve, the schnorkel proved tricky in operation. In all but the calmest seas, a seaman had to be detailed to watch the schnorkel, as the diesels had to be shut off whenever the valve closed. If they were allowed to run on for even a few seconds the diesels could pull oxygen out of the boat's atmosphere, causing severe decompression with accompanying ear and breathing difficulties. Burst eardrums were common. The only way to maintain more or less continuous operation of the diesels was to limit a schnorkeling U-boat to 6 kts (1½ kts slower than it could move on its electric drive).

While the schnorkel did offer a U-boat great immunity from Allied anti-submarine measures, it turned it into a slow, blind, largely ineffective weapon. Here the loss of three years of planning and development was most keenly felt. Only now were plans being made to produce, in the type XXI, a boat that could truly take advantage of the potential of the schnorkel.

The type XXI went to sea with a vastly improved schnorkel. Being periscopic, it was designed to run higher above the water, giving much better rough water performance. Also, it was fitted with an automatic shut-off switch that solved the diesel run-on problem. With these improvements, the type XXI could schnorkel safely at 12 kts.

U-889, a type IXC, shows its schnorkel in retracted position in the deck casing. The venting that led to the engine compartment was permanently attached to the tower, only the schorkel tube itself raising or lowering.

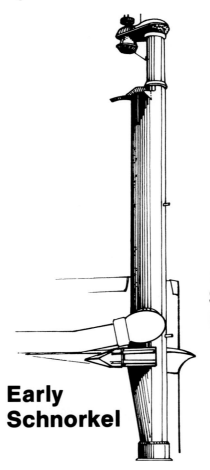

Late Schnorkel Head

Early Schnorkel

In the hands of dockyard workers, U-235 (type VIIC) completes modifications. The schnorkel is seen here in raised position. Being out of commission for refit, the U-boat has been reassigned to the 1.U-Flottille, a training unit, and carries that unit's diablo insignia on its radar housing.

Realizing the vulnerability of their French bases, the Germans began to "harden" their docking and repair facilities in 1941. By the time the Allies got around to bombing the ports in late 1942, the main bunkers were complete and despite saturation bombing at regular intervals, almost no U-boats were lost in these ports. (Above) With its famous dragon insignia faintly visible, U-404 sails in front of the bunkers in one of the French ports. Note the 12 foot thick roof that accounted for their safety. The type VIIC has one of its foredeck torpedo stowage containers angled open. (Bundesarchiv) (Above Right) The view from inside at an approaching type VIIC, U-89. The "Happy Times" are now over and many U-boats return with no successes, as is the case here, to a frequently much less enthusiastic reception. (Bundesarchiv) (Below Right) The reception of a more successful boat gives a good view of the interior of the bunkers. (Bundesarchiv) (Below) A few of the bunker bays were so designed that they could be used as drydocks, keeping the entire repair and resupply facilities beyond the reach of Allied bombing. So effective was this construction that despite attacks by specially designed "Blockbuster" bombs, the ports remained operational until captured by Allied land forces after Normandy. (Bundesarchiv)

Rockets

As was the case in many other fields of advanced experimentation, the Germans only toyed with adapting rockets for launch from a submerged U-boat. It was an idea that was tremendously ahead of its time, as neither the U-boat nor the rocket had at that stage reached the capabilities they would later. Yet, as was the case in other areas, the experimentors did not lack for imagination and in the process set the pattern for weapons that would come into use decades later.

The idea of rocket-firing U-boats came into existence because of a lucky coincidence. It happened that Kvtkpt. Fritz Steinhoff, captain of U-551, had a brother, Dr. Ernst Steinhoff, who was working on small rocket guidance at Peenemünde. After much discussion, they became convinced of the practicality of the idea of mating their two lines of endeavor. During the Summer of 1942, U-551 had a rack for six 30 cm rockets installed, and considerable "unofficial" testing was carried out. These concluded with the successful launch of a rocket from a depth of 12 meters. Yet they were unable to interest anyone on Dönitz' staff and the idea died for lack of official support.

During 1943, the idea arose to launch A-4 (V-2) missiles from submarine-carried, watertight launch containers. A contract for three such containers was given to a Stettin shipyard in December 1944, but none had been completed at war's end.

30cm Wurfkörper 42 Spreng

Two photographs showing the installation and testing of rocket equipment on U-551. All the equipment is Army-issue, 30cm Wurfkörper 42 Spreng rockets then under development, firing from a Schweres Wurfgerät 41 launcher. The rocket was an unguided saturation-type weapon. The technology that would allow successful submarine launched tactical missiles was still 30 years in the future.

A type VIID, U-218, after final pre-commissioning work at Germania Werft, Kiel, on 17 August 1942. The chief distinguishing characteristic of the D series was the hull section with mine tubes added aft of the tower, partially hidden in the shadows. The D's were a particularly successful group, being big enough to carry a barrage of 15 mines while retaining the type VII's maneuverability and rapid diving. U-218 laid a minefield off Lizard Head in August 1944 which claimed one of the war's last victims, a fishing trawler being sunk two months after war's end.

U-213 entering Brest harbor in April 1942. The housing for the above deck extension of the five vertically disposed mine tubes can readily be seen. (Bundesarchiv)

A view of one of a rarely photographed series, U-1060, a type VIIF. One of only four, this boat shows the distinguishing characteristics of the sub-type. The widened deck casing with torpedo handling rails resulting from the added hull section for torpedo stowage.

Type IX

Type IXA (8); Type IXB (14); Type IXC (143); Type IXD (2);

Type IXD2 (30)

The type IXA was an enlarged type I which could trace its antecedents back to the U-81 design of World War I. At just over 1,000 tons, it was the German equivalent of the US Fleet-type or Royal Navy "T" class submarines which were to be the main wartime designs of those navies. With greater displacement and length, the IXs carried bigger machinery and greater stowage than the type VIIs, making them faster and giving them almost double the range. Their greater size, however, made them wetter, less maneuverable and slower diving, earning them the nickname "Seekuh" (Sea Cow). They had a large flat deck casing which completely hid the saddle tanks, distinguishing them from type VIIs.

The type IXBs, which as a sub-type sank more tonnage per boat than any other, were visually indistinguishable from the IXA, differing only with increased bunkerage giving greater range.

The type IXC had greatly increased external stowage giving half again the radius of action. German records class some of these boats as type IXC/40 but disagree as to what made them differ from the earlier Cs. They were visually identical to the Cs, or for that matter, the Bs. Some late C/40s had the deck casing cut away forward in an attempt to reduce the diving time of these big boats.

The type IXDs were an enlarged version of the IXC intended for cargo transport. As such it was without torpedo tubes and most of its battery capacity. As a trade-off it was given more powerful, fast-running diesels to give it higher surface speed, but these proved unsatisfactory and were replaced by standard units. They were nicknamed, not too surprisingly, "Überseekuh" (Overseas Cow).

The sub-type IXD2 was simply an up-powered, armed version of the IXD. It had double the radius of action of the smaller IXCs and could carry an impressive arsenal of mines and torpedoes, but was too unwidely and slow driving to succeed in the hostile Atlantic. Many D2s had the cut-away foredeck casing also, similar to late IXC/40s.

Heavily ice encrusted rather than camouflaged, the first type IXA enters Wilhelmshaven in February 1940. U-37 is seen here flying eight victory pennants, on its way to becoming the sixth most successful boat of the war with over 50 merchant sinkings before being taken off operational status in May 1941. Early type IXs can be recognized by the small deck extensions at the forward gun position. All IX series boats were distinguished by the unbroken line of rectangular free-flooding holes along the side. Note also the exhaust port on the near side aft. (Bundesarchiv)

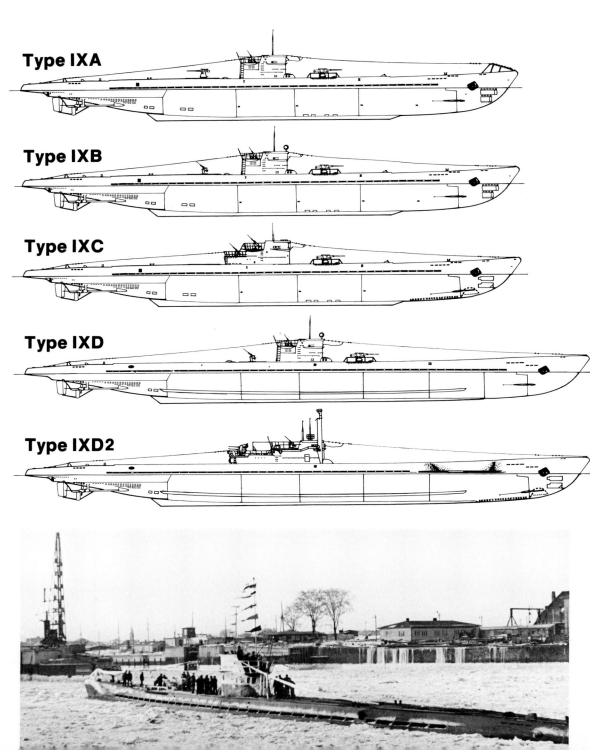

Type IXA

Type IXB

Type IXC

Type IXD

Type IXD2

(Above & Below) Two shots of U-40 (Type IXA) before its first and only patrol. The shot above shows a camouflage and marking similar to that worn by U-25 at the same time. Of particular interest is the variety of early war uniform visible, ranging from standard walking out dress on the left to foul weather gear with leather pants, second from right. Note that the cap band is embroidered "Kriegsmarine" Below, a crewman stands before the open forehatch as the fresh fruit is ready to be loaded aboard immediately before departure. The deck gun, a 10.5cm Schiffs Kanone C/32 in 8.8cm Marine Pivot Lafette C/30D, is clearly shown. (Bundesarchiv)

(Left) A view from directly astern of U-37 entering Lorient shows the smooth curve of the deck casing characteristic of type IXs. In part, the width of this deck, because it trapped air, accounted for the slowness of diving that also characterized the type. (Bundesarchiv)

A clear side view of U-65, type IXB, entering harbor after a patrol, two pennants flying. Visually, it was impossible to distinguish the Bs from the preceding As, the only physical difference being a one foot increase in beam due to increase bunkerage. As a sub-class they were extremely successful, sinking an average of 100,000 tons each, including among their numbers the third through sixth most successful U-boats of the war. (Bundesarchiv)

Another view of U-65, this time being refloated after a time in drydock at Brest in September 1940. Note the four after torpedo stowage compartments in the deck casing, seen here uncovered and empty, between the transfer rails. (Bundesarchiv)

U-103, a type IXB, in harbor undergoing minor repair, camouflage nets being rather haphazardly draped. U-103 was the third most successful boat of the war, being commanded for most of its career by the third most successful commander, Korvettenkapitän Schütze. The boat's insignia, the runic S, represents Schütze's initial. The cover has been removed from the magnetic compass housing. Note also the torpedo trolley on its rails, immediately behind. (Bundesarchiv)

Three views of U-124, type IXB, the fourth most successful boat. (Above) Korvettenkapitän Wilhelm Schulz, under whose command U-124 became famous, is seen on the left with his IWO. Both wear standard issue slickers, but the commander can be distinguished by the fact that his cap has the boat's insignia and he wears the big night binoculars around his neck. (Bundesarchiv) (Below) Two crewmen in standard naval Blue-Grey fatigues stand in front of the boat's insignia on the tower side. The crewman on the left wears leather U-boat pants. (Bundesarchiv) (Right) U-124 entering harbor in Fall 1941 after a successful patrol. Now under the command of Kapitänleutnant Mohr, the boat carries his own insignia, the Green Frog, along with the Edelweiss, as was frequently the case when a new commander took over an already successful boat. (Bundesarchiv)

Under the command of "Kanonier" (Gunner) Lassen, one of the most colorful U-boat commanders, U-160 (type IXC) achieved success in such widely separated areas as the Caribbean, South Atlantic and Indian Oceans. The insignia is that of 10. U-Flottille which operated type IX boats on long range missions from Lorient. The boat is seen here in mid-war pattern, with the added rod antenna and housing. Note the rare additional glass wind screens fitted to this boat. Note also the effect of splinter camouflage on the tower, Medium Grey over Light Grey. (Bundesarchiv)

Pulling into Lorient harbor on 14 September 1942, U-128 (type IXC) is greeted with flowers. Many type IXs, because of their size and sluggishness were identified with animals of similar characteristics. In this case the motto on the side reads "Alter Schimmel, Huahoh, Huahoh" (Old Plowhorse, Giddyap, Giddyap). The boat also carries an unidentified city crest at the front of the tower. Note the Dark Grey camouflage sprayed on the tower side. Note also the swastika emblem affixed to the "Commander's Flagpole", a rare item showing the political inclinations of this particular captain. (Bundesarchiv)

An uncomplimentary and ungracious comparison, the insignia of U-154 represents the nickname of all type IXs, "Seekuh" (Seacow). Launching torpedoes fore and aft with the help of "passing wind", struggling mightily with flippered hooves, she nevertheless demonstrates the affection the crew felt for their boat. Seen here in southern waters, the deck watch is appropriately dressed for tropical sun. (Bundesarchiv)

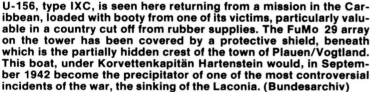

U-156, type IXC, is seen here returning from a mission in the Caribbean, loaded with booty from one of its victims, particularly valuable in a country cut off from rubber supplies. The FuMo 29 array on the tower has been covered by a protective shield, beneath which is the partially hidden crest of the town of Plauen/Vogtland. This boat, under Korvettenkapitän Hartenstein would, in September 1942 become the precipitator of one of the most controversial incidents of the war, the sinking of the Laconia. (Bundesarchiv)

(Above Right) Arriving two days after the sinking of RMS Laconia, U-506, seen here, took a deckload of survivors from U-156. Along with U-507 which arrived the next day, the U-boats attempted to rescue some of the more than 2700 Italian POWs and British passengers who had been on the Laconia. The controversy arose when the U-boats, in this condition and after signalling that a rescue was in progress, were attacked from the air by American bombers. Although over 1000 survivors were landed at French ports, Dönitz issued the "Laconia Order" immediately thereafter, prohibiting the picking up of any survivors by his boats.

Seen at its surrender to the US Navy on 14 May 1945, U-805 displays the late-war form of a type IXC/40. The C/40s differed from the basic Cs primarily in motor fit, but most had the deck casing cut away forward to aid rapid diving, as did most of the later type IXDs. Note, too, the greatly extended Wintergarten with two twin 2cm mounts on the upper level, the folded back shield of a 2cm Flakvierling just visible at the left and the multitude of ready-use containers in between.

Another view of the expanded Wintergarten of a late IXC or D. The actual gun fit varied considerably but the array of eight 2cm seen here was the most common. (Bundesarchiv)

This downward view of the tower arrangement of U-130, a type IXC, shows the essential difference between this and the type VIIs. All the elements are the same, they are just ordered differently. Along the centerline from left to right, are the magnetic compass, periscope standard with holes for scopes plugged, holes in between for short range extendible antennae, the UZO off center to port, tower hatch in front of the periscope standard and surface conning position with voice pipes, compass repeater, engine room telegraph and slot for the retracted FPR. Ventilation shafts come up both side walls, that on the portside with the hole for the long-range rod antenna, while the "Commanders Flagpole", bedecked with flowers and with commissioning pennant flying, is on the port rail. (Bundesarchiv)

U-boats and Aircraft

Having a particularly low superstructure, a submarine has an extremely limited horizon. This is one of the chief limitations of the type, since a U-boat can't sink what it can't see. An observation aircraft was an obvious solution.

Co-operation with shore-based aircraft was useful but was constantly hampered by Göring's intransigence. Out of the range of land, and beyond the political haggling of the Third Reich, the Naval Staff conceived of the need for a U-boat-carried observation aircraft. The idea itself was not new, experiments going on with the Hansa-Brandenburg W20 in 1918. Most naval powers toyed with the idea of at one time or other, particularly the Japanese. Now with the U-Kreuzer of the type XI Class on the drawing boards in 1938, the Arado Flugzeugwerke was given a contract to develop an U-bootsauge (U-boat's eye).

The result of this was the development of the Arado Ar 231. Powered by a lightweight Hirth engine, the little parasol wing float-plane had an endurance of about four hours. The wing center section was angled so that one wing could be stowed above the other when folded back. A set-up and break-down time of six minutes was achieved with the prototypes that were built. First flying in 1941, it proved to have poor airborne and seaborne characteristics. Further, it proved impossible to takeoff in any but the lightest seas. Not too suprisingly, when Dönitz was able to cancel the type XI project, the Ar 231 was dropped by the RLM.

In the meanwhile, another much more novel solution to the problem had been raised. Heinrich Focke, one of the founders of the Focke-Wulf Flugzeugwerke, had been designing autogyros and helicopters since 1932 with some success. Among the designs that had reached production status was the Focke-Achgelis Fa 330 Bachstelze (Wagtail) rotor kite. With the failure of the Ar 231, a search was made for a craft that could be used with existing U-boats. The Fa 330 seemed to be exactly what was needed.

Basically an unpowered autogyro, the Bachstelze operated on the same principals, differing only in that it needed to be towed to stay aloft. The structure was simplicity itself, being nothing more than a vertical pole with a three-bladed rotor at the top and a horizontal pole with landing skids underneath, a seat at the front and fabric-covered control surfaces at the rear. The 18 kt. surface speed of a type IX was sufficient to keep it airborne, being towed by a 150m. cable that included a telephone line. Only seven minutes were required from surfacing of the U-boat for assembly and attainment of 120m. altitude. Recovery proved to be a much slower operation, the tow cable being gradually winched in as the pilot tried to lose altitude. If surprised by an enemy escort ship, the U-boat commander was confronted with the unhappy choice of abandonning the Fa 330 and pilot, which couldn't stay aloft waiting for the boat to surface later, or attempting the dangerously slow recovery process. For this reason, the Fa 330 was unpopular with the U-boats and, even though 200 were built, only a few were used and only in the Indian Ocean where the relative scarcity of both targets and anti-submarine escorts made its use both more helpful and more safe. On at least two occasions, Fa 330s were swapped for the E14Y1 Glen colapsible float planes carried by Japanese I-boats, during encounters in the Indian Ocean. Some of the unfortunate history of Kriegsmarine - Luftwaffe co-operation is told elsewhere, but there was one area where the two forces worked well together. Operating mainly out of Tromsö, Norway, SAGr 130 flying BV138C seaplanes provided excellent reconnaissance of the Murmansk convoy route until the appearance of escort carriers in September 1942, made this too dangerous. As late as August 1943, though, co-operation continued between these planes and the U-boats of the 11.U-bootsflottille. The BV138s were able to double their search range by rendezvousing with the arctic boats, mainly in the protected waters off Spitsbergen, and refuelling for the return sweep. In the most dramatic example of this teamwork during late summer 1943, two U-boats set up a forward base for the seaplanes on the island of Novaya Zemlya, off Russia's Siberean Coast, allowing them to reconnoiter deep into the Kara Sea in search of convoy activity.

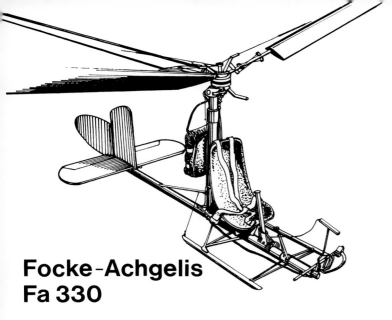

Focke-Achgelis Fa 330

"Flying" on its tether, this Fa 330 Bachstelze trails behind a type IX boat in the Indian Ocean. It was only in those waters that the relative scarcity of targets and escorts made its use more necessary and more safe. Note the number of crew left on deck in case the kite had to be hauled in.

Type X

Type XA (project); Type XB (8)

The projected type XA was to have been a monstrous 2500 ton ocean-going minelayer with mine tubes sited both externally amidships and internally on the centerline. The type was not proceeded with because of Dönitz' objections to the great size of the boats.

Eight type XBs, to which Dönitz objected somewhat less, were built. At 1760 tons they were the largest U-boat type completed by the Kriegsmarine. In design they were diminutives of the type XA, but by careful reworking of the plans they were made capable of carrying more mines, a total of 66, as well as two stern torpedo tubes. They were, however, almost never used in their intended role, most of them having storage containers mounted over their external mine shafts, and being used as supply U-boats. It was a duty for which they were woefully unsuited, but the failure of the surface supply system made their use as such necessary.

Type XB

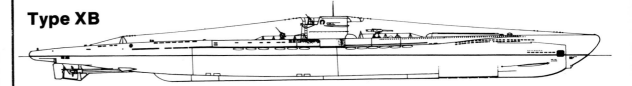

Seen in harbor at Kiel in the fall of 1942, U-119, a type XB, has already been modified away from its original intent. Although the six mine tubes forward, similar in arrangement to those on a type VIID, were still useable, all 24 external shafts on the beam were rendered inoperative by the presence of four torpedo storage containers on either side. The T-shaped apparatus in front of the mine tube housing is the "accoustic hammer" hydrophone set. (Bundesarchiv)

Type XIV

Type XIVA (10); Type XIVB (project)

The first of the war-time designs to reach production, the type XIVs were supply subs, designed from the outset as such, intended to replace the modified attack-type IXDs and the converted minelayer type XBs. As such, the "Milchkuh" (Milk Cow) was designed with a shorter, fuller hull than the earlier types, with increased external bunkerage. These boats suffered the disadvantage of any submarine of that size, being very slow to submerge.

Ten were launched in two groups, the six boats of the first group having some success until the combined efforts of Allied code-breaking and air search caused the loss of three in a six day period in July 1943. Only the four of the second group that had been launched were completed. The remaining ten were broken up on the slipways and all future orders cancelled.

There was a project for an enlarged type XIVB which was cancelled at the same time as the remaining type XIVAs.

Type XIVA

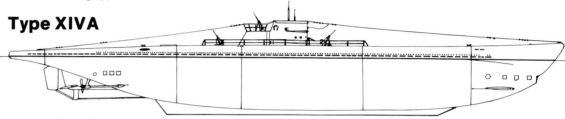

A resupply rendezvous, the kind that made the Western Atlantic available to the limited range type VIIs such as U-132 in the foreground, seen here approaching the "Milchkuh", U-461, in July 1942. Besides the obvious danger of operating two small boats in close quarters on the high seas, there was added the liability of having so many men on deck in waters increasingly patrolled by Allied aircraft. In a typical encounter in October 1943, U-460 was caught on the surface with three type VIIs, resulting in two boats being sunk and one damaged.

Two more views of U-119 at Kiel, having just finished the modifications to make it a supply U-boat. The four stowage containers were not on the boat as built. In the view below, the scorching from the weld can still be seen around the newly fashioned portside fairings. Note the deceptive camouflage on the hull side, intended to make the massive XB seem smaller and hopefully a less attractive target. (Bundesarchiv)

Type XVII

Type XVIIA (4); Type XVIIB (3); Type XVIIB2, B3, G, E, K (projects)

The design antecedent of the XVIIs was the pre-war type V project. The type V was the first of many unconventional projects to emerge from the Walter design bureau. Dr. Hellmuth Walter was driven by the idea that the U-boat's potential had hardly been explored and that the breed was capable of much greater performance. The V project, which was rejected at the drawing stage, called for a small, type II-size boat to carry almost six times the conventional propulsion, given an estimated under water speed of 30 kts. As with all Walter projects, the type V was meant to exploit the characteristics of Hydrogen Peroxide (H_2O_2) in a stablized form called Perhydrol. This chemical has the ability to break down into water and oxygen ($H_2O + O_2$) which can provide a U-boat with air to run its diesels while completely submerged.

The type XVII designation was used as a catchall title to cover a variety of projects. All they shared in common was that they were imaginative and that they were efforts to produce small U-boats with fast underwater speed. Most of the XVIIs originated with Prof. Walter's design bureau.

The type XVIIs grew out of the earlier type V by way of two transitional designs. The first of these was the VB (later called VB60 or V.60) which was to have been a diminutive, 60 ton version to the type V driven by the new Walter turbine. This new system was similar to that proposed for the type Vs, using Perhydrol as a source of oxygen, differing in how propulsion was gained. Instead of simply using the oxygen derived from the decomposition of Hydrogen Peroxide to run a diesel, the Walter turbine system used the heat as well. Since the result of decomposition was oxygen and steam at over 1700°F, it was possible to use this to ignite fuel oil in a combustion chamber, and to use the resulting stream of exhaust gas and steam to run a turbine. While this may sound complex, the result was a power plant much more compact and lightweight than diesels of similar power and completely independent of an external air supply. The chief disadvantage of the system was that it used tremendous amounts of Perhydrol (a Walter Turbine used 25 times the propellants per mile than a diesel), severely limiting the range of a U-boat powered only by turbine.

Even on the drawing boards, the VB was recognized as being too small to be an effective test vehicle for the new propulsion unit. It was replaced by a new design, V.80, which was built, having been launched 19 January 1940, and tested extensively. At 80 tons, it was no more than an unarmed experimental craft, never commissioned into the Kriegsmarine. The V.80 had its share of teething troubles, but it proved the feasibility of the Walter system reaching the unheard of speed of 28 kts submerged.

Following the relative success of the V.80 the first of five different designs that earned the designation type XVIIA was produced, the 650 ton V.300 being proposed in 1941. The plans called for the addition of a small standard diesel to help overcome the limited range of the V.80. This created a new problem. After fitting two complete power plants and the vast amounts of Perhydrol necessary, even after providing a second, semicircular pressure hull under the first, there was little room left over for crew and armament .V.300, renamed U-791, was launched in 1943 but never completed. The second and third type XVIIA designs were proposed improvements of the V.300 which were designated V.300 II and III. Both proposals were dropped in favor of the next design.

The final twos XVIIA designs were similar, both being coastal boats of slightly under 300 tons. Two of each design were completed, though all four had different machinery arrangements. The Wa201 (U-792, U-793) had an underwater speed of 25 kts and a range of 1800 miles on the small supplementary diesels. The Wk202 (U-794, U-795) were slightly smaller, one knot slower and possessed similar range. All four boats carried two bow tubes with one reload for each, and were used operationally. They were limited by their

The experimental boat that led to the development of the Walter-powered type XVIIs, V.80 is seen immediately before launch from Krupp's Germania Werft, Kiel in 1940. Even though it was never commissioned into the Kriegsmarine, it is wearing a very "official" looking Dark Grey over Light Grey camouflage on the tower. Being designed to operate wholly submerged, V.80 displays a very modern hydrodynamic shape.

The second of four boats to be classified type XVIIA, U-793 (Wa 201) is seen here still in dockyard hands in April 1944 in front of the Blohm und Voss yard, Hamburg. Combining a Walter turbine with conventional diesel-electric propulsion, and armed with two torpedo tubes, this was one of the first class of true military submarines.

still small radius of action and the uncertain supply of Perhydrol.

Following the successful completion of trials by the XVIIAs, an order went out for a larger class of slightly enlarged XVIIBs. Bigger by about 40 tons, almost all of which went toward greater oil fuel stowage, they were marginally slower but had nearly double the range. Three of the 12 ordered were eventually put in service, two more were fitting out, while the remaining seven were cancelled. Enthusiasm for the design began to slip when it was realized that they still offered little in the way of offensive punch, were phenomenally expensive to build and operate and still depended on a questionable supply of propellant. Here, perhaps more than any other sector of U-boat construction or preparation, the Allied Strategic Bomber offensive had an effect.

Type XVIIB2 and B3 designs were proposed, but met with a cool reception for the same reasons that the original B series was never completed. Similarly, 12 boats of the XVIIG design were ordered and laid down but soon cancelled.

Two final designs emerged under the general heading of type XVII which were attempts to achieve increased underwater capabilities without the Walter turbine. The type XVIIE (for "Elektro" - Electric) would have replaced the Walter turbine with a more powerful electric motor and increased battery stowage, but as the similar type XXI and XXIII designs were in the works, the E was not pursued. The type XVIIK (for "Kreislauf" - Closed Cycle) would have replaced the Walter system with a much more powerful diesel, and the Perhydrol stowage with oxygen cylinders. Instead of the complex process of Perhydrol breakdown, the K would simply have used stored oxygen to run the diesels submerged. While it promised no better underwater range than the Walter boats, it did offer the advantage of not being dependent on the inconsistent supply of Perhydrol. Three unarmed, experimental boats were ordered, U-798 being launched in February 1945, but never completed.

In spite of the qualified success of previous Walter designs, the need for an improved replacement for the type VIIs was such that Dönitz pressed for an enlarged, ocean-going version of the basic type XVII. Growing out of Walter's Pr. 476 design, the type XVIII would have been about 1600 tons, making them identical in size to the type IXDs but with less than a quarter the range. On the other hand, while a type IXD was capable of not quite seven knots submerged, the type XVIII would have done 24.

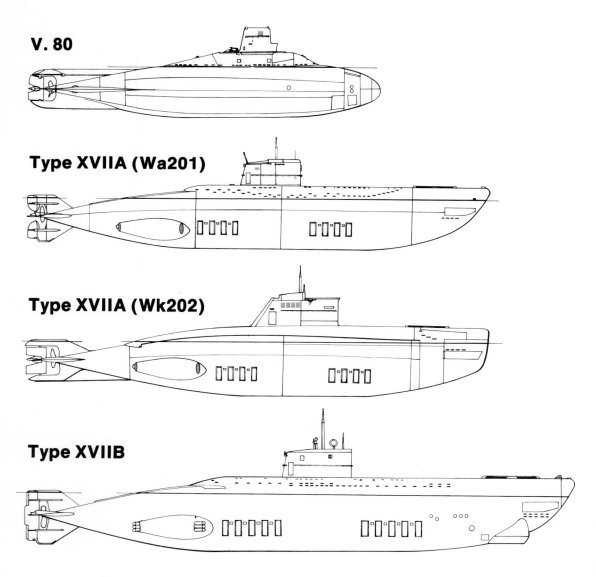

V. 80

Type XVIIA (Wa201)

Type XVIIA (Wk202)

Type XVIIB

U-794 (Wk 202) being "launched" by crane at Germania Werft, Kiel on 7 October 1943. The third type XVIIA, built to the second pattern, it shows the evolution of hull shape in search of designs maximized for efficiency underwater rather than on the surface.

Type XXI

Type XXIA (121) type XXI B, C, D, V, E, T (Projects)

In September 1942, a conference was held, attended by Dönitz, Hitler and Dr. Walter that was to have immense import. At that meeting, Dönitz predicted the defeat of the following May and demanded that all efforts be put to mass-production of Walter's Pr. 476 (type XVIII). Hitler was enthusiastic and gave his approval. By November however, it was becoming obvious that mass-production of type XVIII boats was out of the question and after two prototypes were ordered, remaining plans were shelved. The project may have gotten no further than that, had not the director of the Marinebau, a Prof. Oelfken, come up with an alternative. In April 1943, he submitted detailed plans for converting the basic type XVIII design, with minimum alteration, into an "Elektroboot" (Electric Boat).

The type XXI, as the design was called, simply replaced the double power plant of a type XVIII with the lightweight diesels as fitted to type VIIC/42s and the Perhydrol stowage in the lower half pressure hull with storage batteries. The end result was a boat the size of a type IXD (the largest operational German attack submarines) but of immensely greater ability. While the XXI had only about half the range of the earlier type (11,000 miles) and a marginally slower surface speed (15 kts), it was designed to excell under the surface. Indeed, it was faster submerged than not. Capable of bursts of 17 kts speed submerged, and of schnorkelling at 12 kts, as compared to seven and six for the earlier type, it could drive deeper by a margin of 100m to a depth of 300m and stay down longer. a type IXD was designed to remain submerged for a maximum of 14 hours, while the XXI could stay down for 48 hours at normal speed or 11 days at economical creeping speed without so much as raising a schnorkel.

Being intended as the world's first operational class of true submarines (ie: boats designed from the outset to operate continuously submerged) they were equipped for their task. They were air conditioned and fitted with a garbage disposal system so that the air remained breathable. They had a freezer so that fresh meat and vegetables could be served to the crew. They were even equipped to make war totally submerged. Fitted with hydrophones of a range of 50 miles, a sophisticated echo chamber (Balkon Gerät) which could track, identify and range multiple targets while totally submerged, and an impressive array of torpedoes, the type XXI was intended to attack without coming closer to the surface than 50m. It seemed that they possessed the qualities necessary to turn the Battle of the Atlantic back in the favor of the Germans, and as such were ordered into immediate mass-production by Dönitz.

The first prototypes were ordered while OKM began to work up a program of construction that called for 12 boats a month by August 1945. Dönitz objected vehemently, claiming this would give him too few boats too late. Turning to Armaments Minister Albert Speer, a program of component construction was developed by Speer's assistant, Otto Merker. The Merker plan called for the pre-assembly of the boats in eight sections, being joined together on the building slip in a minimum of time. It was anticipated that each boat would spend only 30 days in the assembly yard. The plan called for the delivery of 33 boats a month from three yards beginning in October 1944. But detail drawings went out to the yards late. Being hurried they were sometimes incomplete or incorrect, causing some final assembly problems, and the two main diesel suppliers were suffering frequent Allied bombing. By July instead of 18 boats being delivered, only one actually was turned over, U-2501, which had to be returned to the yard for immediate repair. The new type had its share of teething troubles, but on the whole, came into service as smoothly as any equally revolutionary project.

A type XXI at launch from A G Weser, Bremen, an example of the first class of true ocean-going military submarines. Designed for minimum visibility while submerged, it and all other late type U-boats are painted overall Dark Grey. While they were envisioned as the "Wolfpack" boats of the future, they were more than double the size of their predecessors, the type VIIs.

This view of one of the pre-fabricated sections of a type XXI on the dockyard trolleyway shows the "figure 8" cross-section characteristic of the Walter design from which it originated. The larger top section was used for power plant, armament and crew, while the lower half section was for fuel and battery storage.

A rare view of a type XXI on the surface, really out of its element, seen here off the coast of Norway where all operational XXIs were based. Now that U-boats were intended to operate wholly submerged, the practice of painting on an insignia was discontinued.

The first boat was coming ready for operational service in March 1945, U-2516, while another 30 were in stages of trials and training. A number of boats, including U-2516, were lost at dockside during strategic raids on Hamburg, only two boats actually leaving on operational patrol, U-2511 (Kvtkpt. Schnee) and U-3008 (Kptlt. Manseck). Leaving for operations in the Caribbean on 30 April 1945, Schnee was under orders not to engage enemy vessels during the outbound voyage. Nevertheless, he encountered and carried out a mock attack on the heavily protected HMS Norfolk, escaping without detection. The end of the war forced his return to base where there were now 12 boats fully ready for action.

It is idle speculation to debate the potential effect of the type XXIs on the Underwater War. What can be stated is that there were 121 in the water at War's End with over 1000 on order or under construction. They could not have failed to make the Battle of the Atlantic more interesting for everyone involved.

U-3505 shows the overall streamlined form of the design. The enclosed automatic twin turrets were a further attempt to keep water resistance to a minimum. Designed to use the new Army developed 3cm Flak 103/38, all type XXIs were in fact fitted with standard 2cm Flak when the larger gun proved slow in materializing. All periscopes, radar and radio antennae and detectors and schnorkel retract into the tower structure.

Type XXI

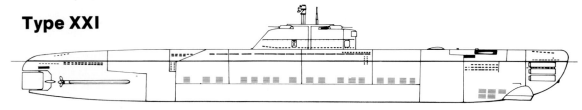

Type XXIII

Type XXIII (59)

The type XXIIIs were the last-designed full-size boats to be completed. They were small coastal diminutives of the "Elektro" design weighing about 230 tons, being roughly equivalent in size to the pre-war type IIAs. Comparison between the two raises the same points as the comparison between types XXI and IXD2. The type XXIII was slower on the surface, almost twice as fast submerged, with more than five times the underwater endurance. The primary disadvantage of the type was that internal space was so cramped that no reloads for the two torpedo tubes were carried and those had to be loaded externally.

Even though design of the XXIIIs at Merker's Gluckauf (Good Luck) Deisgn Bureau was not begun until work on the XXIs was complete, the later type was in the water and in operation sooner. By February 1945, when the first XXIII left for operations around the British Isles, there were close to 50 in the water. Eventually, six type XXIIIs would leave on war patrols, none being sunk. The last of them, U-2336 under Kptlt. Klusmeier, scored the last U-boat victories of the war, two British freighters sunk inside the Firth of Forth on 7 May 1945. 59 type XXIIIs had been launched by War's End, with another 900 under construction or ordered. Nevertheless, the type was always secondary in Dönitz' plans to the type XXI, because its limited range and armament restricted its offensive potential.

Type XXIII

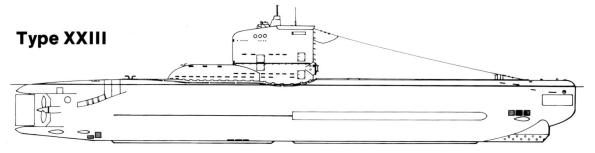

(Below) U-2360 being put into the water at Deutsche Werft, Hamburg. Basically diminutives of the type XXI, the type XXIIIs were fast and elusive but lacked the offensive punch necessary to be really effective. Note the total lack of deck casing and the Balkon Gerät beneath the bow. (Left) U-4707 in harbor immediately after its commissioning on 20 February 1945, showing its smallness in relation to the crew members visible on its bridge.

The bow sections of two type XXIs being looked over by a British soldier after the capture of the Hamburg yard of Blohm und Voss in May 1945. The boat in the background has its forward torpedo tube doors closed, while that in the foreground has them open. Note also the massive echo chamber, "Balkon Gerät" (Balcony Device), under both bows.

Submarines and Sub Hunters

4002 U.S. Subs

4008 FLETCHER DDs

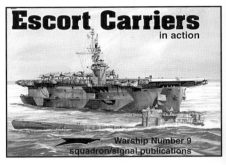

4009 Escort Carriers

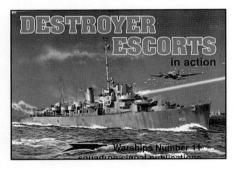

4011 Destroyer Escorts

1074 PBM Mariner

1080 B-24 Liberator

8260 B-25 Mitchell in Detail

1082 TBM/TBF Avenger

8264 B-24 Liberator in Detail

from squadron/signal publications